THE
BEST
HUSBAND
EVER

*The Challenge of Loving
Like Jesus*

THE
BEST
HUSBAND
EVER

*The Challenge of Loving
Like Jesus*

Aubrey Johnson

Cecil May Jr.

Lonnie Jones

Ben Hayes

GOSPEL
ADVOCATE

A TRUSTED NAME SINCE 1855

Published by Gospel Advocate Co.
1006 Elm Hill Pike, Nashville, TN 37210
www.gospeladvocate.com

ISBN: 978-0-89225-665-5

DEDICATION

To Lisa, Winnie, Jacque and Kenya –
our best friends and the best wives ever.

Other Books by Aubrey Johnson

The Barnabas Factor: Realize Your Encouragement Potential

Renewing Your Spiritual Life

Music Matters in the Lord's Church

Spiritual Patriots: Jude's Call to Arms

Love More, Sin Less: Developing a God-Shaped Heart

The Seed Principle: Sowing the Life of Your Dreams

God's Game Plan: Strategies for Abundant Living

Dynamic Deacons: Champions of Christ's Church

Other Books by Cecil May Jr.

Providence: The Silent Sovereignty of God

Bible Questions and Answers

TABLE *of* CONTENTS

ABOUT
This Book

When you become a Christian, two wonderful things happen. First, Jesus' blood removes your sins to give you a fresh start in life (Ephesians 1:7). Second, His teaching renews your mind so you don't have to repeat the same mistakes over and over again (Romans 12:2). The quality of your thinking determines the quality of your life, and that includes your married life. Your marriage will be more successful if you spend more time thinking about your wife than yourself. To borrow from a familiar quote, "Ask not what your wife can do for you. Rather, ask what you can do for your wife." By thinking unselfishly, responsibly and graciously, you can experience a little heaven on earth in your home.

Most people think happiness in marriage depends on ideal circumstances. Jesus knew that happiness is a choice. You do not wait for it. You create it. How? One holy thought at a time. Developing the mind (mental habits) of Christ is the foundation for a great marriage. When her heart beats in your chest, the rhythm of love will bring you more joy than you ever thought possible; but if you cannot feel her heart, you are suffering from a hard heart (Hebrews 3:13).

Being the best husband ever is not a claim but an intention (Philippians 3:12). It is not arrogant but aspirational. It is what a Christian husband longs for and strives for his entire lifetime. This is the power of faith, hope and love at work in your marriage. These holy qualities create new realities from intense longings and persistent prayers.

To have the best possible marriage, something has to change and that something is you. If you hold onto who you are, you cannot become who you were meant to be and who she needs you to be (Matthew 16:25). Give up your worldly ideas of marriage and manhood and embrace Christ's ideals. When you start thinking about your wife the way Jesus thought about His bride, the church, marvelous things will happen.

Marriage provides you with plenty of motivation, opportunity and feedback for growth. As you become a better husband, you will automatically become a better human being. Spiritual growth and self-improvement flow naturally from a loving heart. By caring for your wife, you become a caring person; and by serving her, you become servant-hearted. You cannot be your best without being her best.

If you think everyone is lying and cheating and out for himself in marriage, think again. Plenty of men just like you want to be true and faithful to their spouses. Multitudes understand that life is about rewarding relationships rather than amassing money or chasing pleasure. They are dedicated to blessing their families and glorifying God by serving those they love.

The men who teamed up to write this book want to join you in your challenge to be the best husband ever. When we began this project, we decided to choose co-writers from different generations and backgrounds. We hope the variety of our life experiences will add to the richness of this book and your enjoyment of it. No matter how young or old you are, now is the perfect time to take your love to a higher level.

We want to walk with you through this journey, so here is our pledge to you. First, we promise to spend every day of this partnership asking ourselves, "How can I be the best husband ever?" Second, we promise not to dish up platitudes, but to honestly look for ways we can improve as husbands and then share our discoveries with you. Third, we promise to pray about this like our souls and families depend on it. And fourth, we promise to work on ourselves to see how we can change rather than demand that our wives change to suit us.

A Christlike Husband's
HEART

"Keep your heart with all diligence,
for out of it spring the issues of life"
(Proverbs 4:23).

Solomon's proverb means when you and your wife are having "issues," the real problem and the real solution resides in your heart. In chapters 1 and 2, you will see how developing a Christlike heart is the key to a happier marriage.

Chapter 1

THE CHALLENGE
Aubrey Johnson

*You cannot have the best
if you do not shoot for the best.*

I magine a marriage where you and your mate are close friends. You talk openly about your hopes and fears. You plan for the future and work together to solve problems that confront you as a couple. You cherish each other's company and schedule date times to protect against the intrusion of lesser priorities. Such a life is not an impossible dream. It is the result of high goals, hard work and holy living.

This book is built on two basic beliefs: First, it is possible to improve your marriage (Philippians 4:13). Second, the key to improving your marriage is improving yourself. Too many men are waiting for their marriage to get better instead of working to make their dreams come true. They hang their hopes for the future on spouse-improvement rather than self-improvement. Complaining about your mate's shortcomings and waiting for her to change is a recipe for marital disaster. Setting a clear goal and following a simple plan has much better prospects for success. The most stubborn truth of life is this: You reap what you sow.

Imagine what will happen when you decide to take the first step and focus all your efforts on becoming the best husband you can be. The going will be slow at first. She may question your sincerity or resolve. No doubt, disappointments and setbacks will come along the way. But what can you expect over the long haul? More joy than you thought was possible on earth; not the shallow temporary joy that comes from being waited on hand and foot, but the deep and lasting joy of servanthood, spiritual growth and satisfying relationships. Your life will matter to others, and what could be more joyous than that?

The Motive

When you have a good reason for doing something, it helps you honor your commitment when the going gets tough. With that in mind, I want to give you some reasons why this challenge is worth the price you must pay.

You Will Please God

Marriage is God's gift to you and tending your marriage is your gift to Him. You please and honor God when you make the most of your marriage. And when you do your best, you are more likely to hear these words of commendation: "Well done, good and faithful servant [husband]; you were faithful over a few things, I will make you ruler over many things. Enter into the joy of your lord" (Matthew 25:21).

As a man, God gives you a few things to oversee during your days on earth; things like caring for your body and your reputation. Caring for your wife is another of those things; yet somehow, this sacred obligation gets pushed to the bottom of your commitments. Yes, you hold down a job, bring home a paycheck, and cut the grass on weekends (occasionally), but somewhere along the way you stopped trying to bring her joy. At one time, it was all you could think of, but now it seldom crosses your mind. Let me ask – did you enjoy life more then or now? Then why not go back to the future? It is not too late to write a new ending to the story of your life. If you won't do it for yourself, do it for the glory of God.

You Will Bless Your Bride

Your reputation is important, but don't do it just for your honor – do it for her. She needs you, and frankly, she deserves better. Even when she is stubborn and difficult, she is silently holding out hope that you will see through her defenses to the woman waiting to be loved and cherished. Will you break her heart again, or restore her hope in the man of her dreams? If you won't do it for yourself, do it for the girl you married.

You Will Inspire Your Kids

Attitudes about marriage are more caught than taught. Without saying a word, you define what is "normal" in the minds of your kids. Your example sets the bar of their expectations, and those expectations create their future reality. Make up your mind to raise the bar by showing them that mutual respect, cooperation and happiness are possible if you diligently work at them. If you won't do it for yourself, do it for your kids.

You Will Improve Yourself

Whether you eloped or your guest list numbered in the hundreds, your vows were registered in heaven for all time. You made a commitment to another human being, the most important one you will ever make. At that moment, she entrusted her hopes and dreams to you as well as her body. You promised to make caring for her your top priority, second only to your devotion to God, and the highest expression of your love for Him.

The world says, "Big deal. Vows are just words imposed on you by religion and social convention." God's Word says that marital faithfulness is a big deal indeed. It is about your soul and your destiny (Matthew 19:9). It is also about your integrity (Numbers 30:2; Deuteronomy 23:21-23; Malachi 2:13-16). On those days when you don't feel like putting forth much effort, do the right thing anyway. Remember, your good name is on the line. And when you keep your vows, you also keep your self-respect.

Here is what you can expect if you give your all to become the best husband ever. You will like yourself more when you look in the mirror each morning. Your self-respect will surge with every effort you make to improve. In time (don't expect overnight miracles), your wife will realize you are serious, and she will begin to warm up and reciprocate your small gestures of selfless love. It will be the hardest thing you have ever done, but it will become the thing you are proudest of in your life. No dusty trophy, fading certificate or past glory can compare with the satisfaction of becoming a Christlike man who lays down his life for one he loves.

The Plan

Paul compared progress in Christian living to running a race. It is also a perfect analogy for moving forward in your marriage.

Do you not know that those who run in a race all run, but one receives the prize? Run in such a way that you may obtain it. And everyone who competes for the prize is temperate in all things. Now they do it to obtain a perishable crown, but we for an imperishable crown. Therefore I run thus: not with uncertainty. Thus I fight: not as one who beats the air. But I discipline my body and bring it into subjection, lest, when I have preached to others, I myself should become disqualified. (1 Corinthians 9:24-27)

The competitors in a race push each other to give their best effort. Paul understood that only one person can cross the finish line first, but there is great honor in giving your maximum effort. Paul is talking about the benefits of a goal-directed life. Preparation is the key to performance in marathons and marriage.

Corinth was the site of the Isthmian Games. Athletes would plan their training regimen and follow it religiously in hopes of attaining the victor's prize. Paul admired their grit and challenged Christians to show the same determination in pursuing spiritual goals. Every life choice must become subordinate to your higher purpose. As a Christian husband, the victor's prize is no mere laurel wreath. It is winning your wife's heart. No worldly reward can ever compare with how it feels when you gain her trust and respect. Growing to become that man is what this book is all about.

When it comes to building an incredible marriage, most men display little forethought or effort. To use Paul's terminology, they run with uncertainty. It seems like they have no plan or goals. They just go through the motions, not getting any better and often getting worse. To be a truly great husband, you need to get serious about life and be ready to sacrifice anything that interferes with your aim. Achieving your objective will require focus and discipline.

The Little Things

What is your plan for having the best possible marriage? One key to happiness is making small daily changes in yourself to bring more joy to your wife. In other words, the practical path to improving your marriage is improving yourself. When you start thinking this way, every day becomes an adventure as you search for little ways to please your spouse.

For example, I used to get in trouble for not putting a liner back in the kitchen trash can after carrying the trash outside. I always meant to, but somehow I would get distracted and forget. Telling my wife, Lisa, about my good intentions was not convincing, especially after the 50th time. Then I discovered a simple solution that has worked wonders for our marriage. I decided to put the new liner in the can before I carry the trash outside. I pull the full bag out of the bin, tie it off, set it against the side of the can, and replace the liner immediately. Voilà! Instant brownie points. And by reducing the number of little irritations I inflict on my wife, I am the beneficiary of her smiles and goodwill. Besides improving her day, I have earned her respect because she knows I love her. How does she know? Because I am trying to bring her joy.

So ask yourself, "What do I have a habit of doing that irritates my sweetie?" Is it leaving dirty clothes around the house? Leaving the gas tank on empty? Leaving the lid up? Leaving the house at the last minute? Leaving dirty dishes everywhere? Leaving without a kiss? Look for recurring behaviors to get the biggest return on investment. Once you identify the opportunity for improvement, think hard and come up with a simple, permanent solution that will require some discipline but probably not a lot of effort. The next step is deliberate practice, and every time you go the second mile, you are reminding her she is adored and treasured.

Happiness in marriage has less to do with diamonds and fancy dinners than with kindness and consideration. Give attention to the little things, and you will reap big rewards. Think of yourself as the Sherlock Holmes of marital happiness, and start searching for ways to delight your darling. The clues are there. All you have to do is care enough to notice.

The Best Husband Ever

To be the best husband ever means you are committed to becoming the best husband you can be. It is less about comparing yourself with other men and more about striving to exceed your past efforts as a husband. It is pressing toward the mark of the high calling of God (Philippians 3:14) in holy matrimony. Successful husbands are driven by a never-ending desire to improve themselves. Every day, they look for a new way to bless the one they promised to care for during their lifetimes on earth.

However, to become your absolute best, one comparison is essential. Paul challenged husbands to emulate Christ's devotion to His bride, the church (Ephesians 5:25). Without question, Jesus was the best husband ever. His relationship with the church is the greatest love story ever told. Therefore, the more Christlike you are, the better husband you become. In the following chapters, we will examine qualities from Christ's life that can take your marriage to the next level. And when faced with difficult choices, there is a question that will shed light on the best way forward. "What would Jesus do?" Or better yet, "What did Jesus do?" Husbands who follow in Jesus' footsteps will enjoy a more abundant life and a more rewarding marriage.

To shoot for best is different than better. The goal is not a little change to satisfy a nagging conscience. Rather, it is reaching for the stars. A man who longs to be his best asks a whole different set of questions than someone who is trying to get his wife off his back. His passion for improvement is extraordinary. Half-measures will not do. Settling is not an option. Supreme effort is essential. Greatness is the goal (Matthew 23:11). You cannot have the best if you do not shoot for the best.

Imagine how your wife will feel when she notices how hard you are trying to improve yourself and your marriage. Think of the joy she will experience when you repeatedly go the second mile to meet her needs. Envision what could happen if her gratitude for your attention and kindness starts a positive chain reaction where you constantly try to outdo one another in higher expressions of love (Romans 12:10).

Are You Ready?

Jesus warned His followers to "count the cost" before committing to any course of action (Luke 14:28). In the interest of full disclosure, we want to warn you that taking the best husband ever challenge will be the most demanding thing you have ever done. But if you are tired of settling for scraps of marital happiness, we can show you the way to the marriage of your dreams (1 Corinthians 12:31).

The first step to becoming the best husband ever is to become a Christian. God commands it, and love demands it. Jesus is the ultimate source of marital wisdom; make Him the Lord of your marriage. When you emerge from the waters of baptism, you will be a new man and take your first step on the path to becoming a more loving husband.

Jesus will not only bless you eternally but maritally. He can save your soul and your home as well. If you are ready to quit complaining and start changing, we want to introduce you to the man whose example will inspire you to rethink your approach to marriage, the best husband ever, Jesus Christ.

HONEY-DO LIST: Item #1
Take The Best Husband Ever Challenge

1. What is your reason for taking the best husband ever challenge?

2. How will you know if you succeed?

3. What will it feel like?

4. When your wife knows she is cherished, how will she feel?

5. How will she respond?

6. How will it benefit your children?

7. How will it glorify God?

8. How will it bless you?

9. If you knew you could not fail, would it be worth the cost?

10. Why is becoming a Christian the first step to being your best?

Powering Up

Real and lasting change is not easy. In fact, you cannot do it on your own. You need God's help, the kind available in prayer. At the close of each chapter, you will be encouraged to "power up" by praying for your marriage. This week, ask God to help you become your best self.

Marriage Magic

The magic of marriage is imagining ways to bring your spouse joy and then following through on your plans. In this section, we will suggest a weekly activity to demonstrate your love and draw your hearts closer together. The key is to be creative and enthusiastic. This week, arrange a time for a serious discussion with your wife. Tell her you are taking a challenge to work every day at becoming the best husband you can be. You may want to apologize for taking so long to grow into the man of her dreams. Next, ask her to tell you one thing you could do to bring more joy to her life. When you get your answer, write it down, post it where both of you will see it every day, and go to work. Do not skip the writing and posting, and do not delay. Convince her of your devotion by your deeds rather than words. Judge yourself by your actions and not just your intentions.

Chapter 2

THE MODEL
Aubrey Johnson

*Jesus is the ultimate model of holy
and committed love.*

The Bible uses many comparisons to help readers understand the relationship between Jesus and His church. He is like a king, priest, cornerstone, shepherd and vine. Of all the endearing portraits showing the connection between Christ and His church, none can compare with the image of a devoted groom and His cherished bride. The marriage analogy speaks of love, protection, generosity, joy – and more than a little suffering. Marriage is the best illustration of commitment to Christ because it is the closest relationship most people experience during their lifetimes.

The Happy Groom

In the gospels, John the Baptist introduced Jesus as "the bridegroom." John saw his own ministry as that of a best man assisting his friend on His wedding day (John 3:29). He knew that the spotlight belongs on the man getting married. Groomsmen are there to serve their brother on his big day.

The term "bridegroom" applies primarily to the day of the wedding ceremony. John compared Jesus' three-year ministry to a single day of preparation for marriage. On their wedding day, a bride and groom are permanently joined as one. They are no longer two but a twosome. People speak of them as a couple, and they see themselves as inseparably linked. This is the way Christ feels about the church. He is passionately and eternally committed to caring for her needs.

In the gospels, we are impressed by the devotion of a woman who washed Christ's feet with tears, kisses and perfume (Luke 7:36-50). However, that story pales in comparison with Jesus who gave not only His tears but His blood to wash our sin-stained souls (Revelation 1:5). Jesus is the ultimate model of holy and committed love.

It is no accident that Jesus' return is portrayed as a bridegroom coming to claim His betrothed on their wedding day (Matthew 25:1-13). We are betrothed to Jesus individually on the day of our conversion (2 Corinthians 11:2), but His people are joined to Him collectively and eternally at His second coming. At that time, the New Jerusalem will be let down from heaven as a bride adorned for her husband (Revelation 21:2). By becoming a Christian, you are privileged to partake in this holy union and to learn from the best how to treat your own bride.

The Worthy Goal

God intended marriage to improve two people's lives by blending their personalities and combining their energies. The spiritual and practical benefits are immense. As faith, hope and love intermingle, blessings multiply to the couple and to those with whom they come in contact. Marriage relieves suffering, renews hearts and refines souls.

Unfortunately, marriage can also be discouraging and destructive when a person is yoked with someone unsuited for matrimony (2 Corinthians 6:14). A man who is cynical and selfish has an adverse effect on his bride. His doubts about the Lord, negativity about life and obsession with self drain the joy from the relationship. Rather than lightening her load, he makes her emotional and domestic burdens heavier. As he pulls her downward, she must work harder to keep the marriage and her faith afloat. The point is that a happy and successful marriage begins with a good choice, and those who link their lives to Christ have the brightest prospects for satisfaction in life and marriage.

The Best Part

The best part of marriage is not the honeymoon. It is helping each other live well. The joy is in giving and growing rather than getting. The momentary ecstasy of sex is God's way of bonding couples and bringing them back to one another despite differences that could drive them apart. Physical intimacy embeds intense feelings of joy and pleasure deep in your memory. Ideally, those passionate emotions are associated with one person. When this is the case, your feelings for her are uniquely positive and facilitate problem solving and conflict resolution. Without those special feelings, it is much easier to withdraw or walk away.

Still, happy marriages are about more than sexual compatibility. A strong marriage is characterized by devotion to your spouse's well-being. The indissolubility of the relationship is not meant to be a trap (Matthew 19:9). Rather, it incentivizes working on practical solutions to life's challenges. If bailing is not an option, then the only honorable answer is to buckle down and search harder for solutions to the difficult problems confronting you as a couple. The permanence of marriage reflects God's confidence in your ability to handle any test with His help. Jesus modeled this extreme devotion in Ephesians 5:25. He refused to walk away when things got tough.

The Model Husband

A model is an example worthy of imitation. A model citizen or student is someone whose conduct is so commendable it would benefit you to do as he or she does. Jesus was a model husband because those who behold His devotion to the church can better their marriages by following His example. Everything Jesus did during His earthly ministry was deliberate. Every word and action was a ready-made lesson for His disciples and future believers. Jesus not only spoke the word – He was the Word. He not only told the way – He showed the way.

Why is modeling such an effective tool for change? Because seeing is believing. It provides clarity and more than a little inspiration. Christians are saved by the death of Christ and sanctified by the life of Christ. His example fires the imagination and fortifies the will to change in positive ways that would not otherwise be possible. Consider the instances on the next page when Jesus provided a model for successful living.

Jesus' Birth

Jesus' birth in humble circumstances was more than a coincidence. He was born in a manger, not a mansion. His first home was the little town of Bethlehem rather than imperial Rome or proud Jerusalem. His first guests were simple shepherds rather than men of worldly power and distinction. God did not send His Son into the world to enjoy its amenities. He was on a spiritual mission and would not be distracted by the cares, riches and pleasures of this life (Luke 8:14). The facts surrounding His birth were messages reflecting His heavenly purpose and uncompromising values. Likewise, successful couples need to stake out their non-negotiable standards from the very beginning.

Jesus' Baptism

Jesus' baptism was more than a spontaneous event. It was a premeditated pattern for every disciple to follow. John the Baptist realized the awkwardness of administering baptism to One so holy and mighty. What he failed to realize was that this was a supreme teaching moment. The Son of God was modeling humility and obedience by submitting to John's baptism. Being immersed in the muddy Jordan River by the hands of a sinful man spoke volumes about Jesus' commitment to doing God's will. The Christian life begins with submission to God. Similarly, a good marriage always begins with dying to self. Every problem that will threaten your happy home is rooted in selfishness. When troubles arise, get back to basics by remembering your baptism and returning God's will to the forefront of your mind. More humility will solve most marriage problems because openness to correction and counsel are the starting points of learning and self-improvement (James 1:21).

Jesus' Battle

Jesus' battle with temptation in the wilderness was more than a personal struggle. It was a crash course on how to handle sinful urges. Jesus kept His focus on glorifying God rather than gratifying His immediate desires. Temptation is a time of extreme danger but also a time of special opportunity. By putting spiritual priorities above physical longings and placing long-term interests before short-term desires, it is possible to resist temptation. The way to overcome sin is by focusing your attention on God's will and His Word. Jesus knew that Scripture holds the solution to any problem you come across in life. The Bible holds the key to solving problems in a healthy way that honors the

Lord. Consequently, those who want a stable marriage must build on the sure foundation of God's Word (Matthew 7:24).

Christ's example provides the perfect pattern for self-improvement and a satisfying life. Wise husbands look to Jesus for direction and inspiration (Hebrews 12:2). His selfless ministry showed that the key to a successful life is serving others. His calmness in conflict demonstrated the blessings of self-control and the virtue of pursuing peace. A selfish heart destroys homes, but a servant heart strengthens them (James 3:13-18). The key to a happy marriage is caring for your wife rather than contending with her.

Love Suffers Long

Everything Jesus ever said and did is worthy of emulation by men who want to excel as husbands. However, Peter singled out one quality deserving of special attention: His willingness to suffer. "For to this you were called, because Christ also suffered for us, leaving us an example, that you should follow His steps" (1 Peter 2:21). The suffering Peter spoke of is the pain you endure by loving someone. The beauty of love is that it always takes the high road. Retaliation is not an option. In marriage there will be times when you are misunderstood and mistreated. What will you do in return?

Christ showed the best possible response. If you are criticized, do not attack in return. When you get hurt, do not make threats (1 Peter 2:23). There will be days your spouse is not at her best (and vice versa). Do not feel that you have to set things right at that moment. Take consolation in the fact that God knows your heart. By patiently bearing wrongs, you protect the relationship from further damage that will make it harder to resolve the issue at hand. Stopping the destructive spiral of blaming and attacking is crucial to recovery. Do not make things worse because your ego is hurting. Put your focus on safeguarding the relationship and supporting your spouse. Self-control and self-denial are essential qualities of Christlike husbands.

Jesus is our model for every relationship but especially the marriage relationship. Being the best husband you can be will require suffering from time to time. Some pain comes from without as you shield your bride from the ugliness of a sinful world. Still, some of the pain will come from misunderstandings between you and your bride. If the disciples doubted, debated and denied the Lord, you can expect the same treatment from those close to you. From time to time, your motives, integrity and wisdom will be questioned. It hurts to be judged and criticized, but the way forward is not to counterattack or withdraw into a shell. The solution is to follow Jesus by loving more rather than less.

The Worst Pain

Woody Allen once said, "The three rings of marriage are the engagement ring, the wedding ring, and the suffering." Unfortunately, some couples spend their lifetimes inflicting mutual pain. Christian love produces a totally different kind of suffering. It is the pain you feel when you long to do someone good but fall short of your goal. One of the worst pains you can experience is the feeling of regret that comes from knowing you have hurt or disappointed your wife.

When my father-in-law, Gale Hearn, turned 80, he could still recall a painful event that took place half a century earlier. My mother-in-law, Marjorie, had traveled 30 hours to join him where he was stationed in Japan. When she got off the plane in Tokyo, there was no one there to greet her. She was 22 years old, from a small town in southern Louisiana, traveling with her 8-week-old son, and did not speak a word of Japanese. It is a moment he wished he could do over, but life does not work that way. The good news is that he learned a great lesson that day. Unfortunately, some men repeat the same thoughtless behavior and offer weak apologies rather than doing the hard work of change.

The best husband challenge is about making better choices that are less selfish and more Christlike. Behaving graciously toward your spouse requires asking the right question. Always ask yourself, "What is best for her?" When you get the answer, do not hesitate. Debate and delay are Satan's tools for weakening your resolve. Do the right thing, and do it quickly.

The problem, however, is how to avoid always equating what you want with what is best. Most men are skillful in masking the selfishness that underlies their choices. It takes hard work to discern your true motives and put her welfare before your wishes. Those who achieve this level of self-honesty are displaying the mind of Christ.

At its core, marriage is about giving and receiving love. The goals are intimacy and growth. As a result, marriage produces different kinds of pain as well as joy. Growth requires the pain of self-denial, forbearance when hurt, and patience with others. Those who love like Christ go to great pains to understand others' feelings and to bear their burdens. One thing is for certain, when you risk loving like Jesus, you are never alone. The "captain" of your salvation has gone before you and His footprints mark each step along the way (Hebrews 2:9-10). In every decision you make, look to Christ for guidance to live and love better.

Lifetime Learners

Great husbands are continual learners who seek to improve themselves every day. They study their wives to know what brings them joy. They ask men they admire to share their secrets for success as husbands. When selecting a marriage mentor, remember that Jesus said, "By their fruits you will know them" (Matthew 7:20). In other words, do not judge a man by his bragging but by his wife's well-being.

The fruit of faith is a flourishing family where members love and support each other in doing God's will. By listening to the wisdom of older men with proven track-records, you can shorten life's learning curve and speed your progress as a husband. Though you will have many mentors during your lifetime, only one role model is worthy of your unqualified trust. With this in mind, we are ready to proceed to the next section of this book to consider 10 ways you can become a truly Christlike husband.

HONEY-DO LIST: Item #2
Carry a Cross for Her, Not Just a Torch

1. What is the purpose of marriage?

2. What is the best part of marriage?

3. Why is the permanence of marriage a good thing?

4. Describe Christ's commitment to His bride.

5. Describe your commitment to your bride.

6. What does suffering have to do with love?

7. What kinds of pain does love produce?

8. How did Jesus suffer for His bride?

9. When you know love produces suffering, how does that change things?

10. Are you prepared to suffer to become a Christlike husband?

Powering Up

Thank God for sending Jesus to show you how to live and love. Ask for strength to love more rather than less when you are going through times of pain.

Marriage Magic

Make a list of three men you look up to as model husbands. Choose one to have lunch with this week, and ask him to share his secrets for success in marriage. Call another and tell him what his example has meant to you. Write or email the third and tell him about your pledge to be the best husband ever. Ask what advice he can give you as you get started. When you enlist the prayers and encouragement of godly men, you gain the support you need to follow through on your commitment. Take full advantage of the help God readily makes available to those who are humble and wise enough to ask. You may want to share your findings with your wife. She will be thrilled to know you are on a quest to be your best.

A Christlike Husband's
HABITS

"Jesus ... went about doing good"
(Acts 10:38).

Cultivating the mind of Christ is just the first step. Next you must develop the habits of Christ that will consistently bless your bride and strengthen your marriage. Chapters 3 through 12 present 10 habits Jesus had that made Him the ideal husband for His bride, the church. Building better habits may not sound romantic, but it is the secret to sustaining your wife's marital satisfaction. And if you want more spontaneity, make a "habit" of surprising her with inventive displays of your affection.

Chapter 3

BE LOVING
Cecil May Jr.

*Love is an act of will that seeks
what is best for the one loved.*

We husbands want our wives to be submissive. The Bible says, "Wives, submit to your own husbands, as to the Lord" (Ephesians 5:22). But what can a husband do when his wife is not submissive? Call 911? "Hey, my wife won't obey me. Will you send the cops to make her obey?" That, for sure, will get him nowhere. Certainly he must not manhandle her or even yell at her. That can land him in jail, and rightly so.

That reminds us that a wife's submission to her husband is voluntary. It is a decision she makes, not one her husband can make for her. Wives are commanded to submit, and we understand there are consequences for disobeying commands of God. However, God commands and leaves it to her to obey. Nowhere does He say to husbands, "Make your wife obey you" or "Get your wife under control." God's instruction to men is, "Husbands, love your wives" (Ephesians 5:25; Colossians 3:19).

Paul, Timothy and Silas were accused of turning the world upside down by the message they preached (Acts 17:6). The gospel does that. It specifically turns the world's idea of how to pursue happiness in marriage upside down. The worldly go into marriage thinking its purpose is "to make me happy." There are bills to be paid and required time restraints on both husband and wife. Both find there is very little discretionary income and perhaps even less discretionary time. Husbands or wives who try to grab every spare minute and every spare dollar for themselves generate conflict, not happiness.

Under God's plan, a submissive wife has a loving husband. Each looks out for what is best for the other. A wife who submits to her husband is more concerned with his interests than her own. A husband who loves his wife seeks her happiness before his own. When husbands and wives put every discretionary dollar and available minute toward what will bring happiness to their mate, they both end up far happier.

As the wife is commanded to be submissive to her husband, so the husband is commanded to love his wife. The worldly think love cannot be produced on command; it is something to fall into, something felt, and "we can't help what we feel or do not feel." If a husband or wife comes to the preacher's office or the counselor's couch and says, "I don't love her (or him) anymore," that is supposed to be an incontrovertible reason for ending the marriage.

God does not command anything that cannot be obeyed. The standard of a husband's love for his wife is "as Christ also loved the church and gave Himself for her" (Ephesians 5:25). That kind of love is not a romantic feeling or a flutter in the heart. It is an act of will that seeks what is best for the loved one.

Obviously, a husband who loves his wife as God commands cannot be an abusive husband, either physically or emotionally. He cannot hit or harm her. He cannot berate her or say derogatory things to her or about her. To the contrary, he will be patient and kind; he will not envy or boast; he will not be arrogant or rude. He will not insist on his own way or be irritable or resentful (1 Corinthians 13:4-5 ESV).

Love Is Both/And

As a child I was told a story of two little boys, sons of a widowed mother. One was very affectionate, would climb into his mother's lap, often told her he loved her, and would shower kisses and hugs on her, but he was somewhat careless in regard to obedience. The other was not affectionate, rarely said loving words or bestowed kisses, but was very dutiful.

One day a serious event occurred and certain things had to be done to avoid catastrophe. The mother gave precise instructions to both boys. One, characteristically, kissed his mother and assured her he would do exactly as told, but as he started, he ran into some of his friends and dallied, eventually forgetting his assigned tasks. The other started out immediately, did everything exactly as he was told and then, realizing his brother had not finished his tasks, did what his brother was supposed to have done also.

The question was then asked, "Which son do you suppose really loved his mother more?" Rather obviously, the answer was supposed to be, "the obedient one," illustrating John 14:15, "If you love Me, keep My commandments" and 1 John 3:18, "My little children, let us not love in word or in tongue, but in deed and in truth." However, I have never been happy with having to make that choice. Love should not be an "either/or"; it should be a "both/and."

A husband who believes it is not his nature to be affectionate needs to be affectionate anyway. "I love you" gets easier and easier to say with repetition, and it is highly unlikely that it will ever be repeated too often. By the way, we need to say it often not only to our wives but also to our children. Never begin a temporary separation or let a full day go by without saying, "I love you."

The way we best show love to our wives is not necessarily the way we want love shown to us. My wife and I learned that lesson early in our marriage. When I am sick, I want to be babied with constant attention. When Winnie is sick, she wants the necessities like food and medicines taken care of, but then she wants to be left alone to get well. When I treated her like I want to be treated and she treated me like she wants to be treated, it did not work for either of us. It took experimentation and communication for us to learn that lesson.

A man and his wife were having breakfast on their 50th wedding anniversary. He makes her toast as he had done for years, and she suddenly shows she is upset, "For 50 years, you have given me the end pieces, and I am sick of it. I hate the end piece!" Her husband was stunned by her outburst and quietly said, "But I was giving you the end piece because it is my favorite. I thought it would be yours too." Husbands and wives need to find out that sort of thing before 50 years go by.

There is no one-size-fits-all way of successfully assuring our wives of our love that is guaranteed to be appreciated and understood. Some wives like flowers; some do not. Remembering significant dates, like birthdays, anniversaries or Valentine's Day with a card or gift is important, probably to most, but not to all. It takes more perception, sometimes, than some men usually exercise to know what will be recognized as a gesture of love. It is important for every husband to dedicate thought and effort to determine what his wife does appreciate and then to act on it. Men tend to think working hard at their jobs to provide a good living for their families is sufficient proof of their love, but it rarely suffices.

One almost universal way of showing affection is the right kind of touch. Erotic touching in private times that is somewhat playful and not necessarily intended to lead immediately to sex is usually enjoyed and appreciated. Hand holding is a powerful way to show a strong connection. One of the first indications a boy and girl may be interested in one another as more than "just friends" is seeing them hold hands as they walk across campus. Too often what begins as an enjoyable way to show affection for one another is forgotten in marriage as couples tend to take one another for granted. If my wife and I are sitting next to each other, we are probably holding hands. If we are walking side by side, we are likely hand-in-hand. It is often favorably mentioned. A manager of a deli we frequent now greets us with, "How are the love birds this morning?" We do not do it for that purpose, of course; we do it because we like it. It keeps us feeling connected.

When we think of love we usually think of loving someone because they are so lovable. Romantic love is a response to sweetness and beauty (at least perceived beauty). "Hollywood love," we might call it. Friendship love results from mutual interests that bring two or more together to engage in activities they share (golfing buddy or shopping sister love, we might say). Hopefully, both of those kinds of love will be prominent in marriage. We want our wives to be both our lovers and our best friends, but beyond either, for us to love our wives as Christ loved the church is to love them whether they are lovers and friends or not, whether they are nice to us or not. That is God's command to husbands. His love for us is not because we are lovable but because it is God's nature to love. "God is love" (1 John 4:16). The Bible says, "The love of God has been poured out into our hearts by the Holy

Spirit who was given to us. For when we were still without strength, in due time Christ died for the ungodly" (Romans 5:5-6). The kind of love that defines God is expressed in His gift to us of His unique Son. The Holy Spirit pours that love into our hearts by making it known to us through the gospel. We in turn, having been so loved, learn to love (1 John 4:19). Thus we love even our enemies, and that is the love with which we are commanded to love our wives.

However, it is not as stark and one-sided as it may sound. One of the powerful things about showing the love we are commanded to show – loving as Christ loved us – is that it produces the other kinds of love that are also important to marriage. Unconditional love given to a wife almost always is rewarded with respect and submissiveness from the wife. In addition, it produces friendship, romantic awakenings and a growing enjoyment in the other's presence. Positive thinking gurus say, "Fake it 'til you make it." "Fake it" is not the term to use, but it is true that feelings follow actions. If you want to love someone, act like you do and you will. Erotic love is rekindled and friendship love is restored when a husband loves his wife like Christ loves the church. When feelings are not present to produce desired actions, taking the desired actions can produce the wanted feelings.

Sex is an important element in marital love. "Therefore a man shall leave his father and mother and be joined to his wife, and they shall become one flesh" (Genesis 2:24). Jesus says this is what God said about His intent for marriage from "the beginning" (Matthew 19:4). It is equivalent to "One man for one woman for life." When husband and wife become "one flesh," it is God who joins them (v. 6). Scripture says,

> Let the husband render to his wife the affection due her, and likewise also the wife to her husband. The wife does not have authority over her own body, but the husband does. And likewise the husband does not have authority over his own body, but the wife does. Do not deprive one another except with consent for a time, that you may give yourselves to fasting and prayer; and come together again so that Satan does not tempt you because of your lack of self-control. (1 Corinthians 7:3-5)

The King James Version says, "Defraud ye not one the other." The original word has the connotation of taking what rightly belongs to another.

Sex in marriage is a delightful gift of God to husbands and wives. "Let marriage be held in honor among all, and let the marriage bed be undefiled" (Hebrews 13:4 ESV). It is a most unfortunate choice of words when teenagers refer to unmarried sex as "going all the way." What is experienced in the back seat of a car or in a stolen moment in a temporarily unoccupied house between two nervous kids with no lifetime commitment, frightened of pregnancy and troubled by guilt is not "all the way." It is not even one-quarter of the way to the joy of a union between a married couple committed to each other for life, expressing in their union not just lust or infatuation but true and lasting love, knowing they are one in the sight of God and the world.

Husbands and wives are different in many ways, including their sexual needs. Husbands are easily aroused and ready for sex quickly and often. Wives need to be loved and shown affection in non-sexual contexts to be ready for sex. Those are generalities, subject to exceptions, but a wise husband will make good use of that knowledge. A husband and wife giving themselves freely and joyfully to each other in the marriage bed is a God-given delight.

Here is a warning and a difference to be taken into account. When a husband is deprived of sex, he feels ignored and unappreciated. When a wife is feeling ignored and unappreciated, she has difficulty giving herself sexually, as well as in other ways. A husband and wife need to be alert to each other's different needs, looking for clues of the other's feelings and desires, and putting each other's happiness ahead of their own.

HONEY-DO LIST: Item #3

Love Her Like Christ Loves Her

1. How would your wife rank you as a "loving" husband?

   Circle a Number   1 2 3 4 5 6 7 8 9 10 +

2. Why not a lower number?

3. Name three things you could do this week to rank higher in her mind.

4. Which one would most make her feel treasured?

5. How could you go about making this change?

6. What would be the first step?

7. When and where could you begin this week? Be specific. Time? Place?

8. How committed are you to making this change to bring her more joy?

   Circle a Number   1 2 3 4 5 6 7 8 9 10 +

9. If your commitment level is less than a 9, go back to step 3 and be more creative. Find a true win/win solution that won't leave you feeling resentful. If you are miserable, no change will bring her joy.

Powering Up

Pray for God's help in becoming a Christlike husband by becoming more loving. Remember, you can do all things through Christ who strengthens you (Philippians 4:13).

Marriage Magic

Ask your wife when would be a good night this week to have an hour or so of her undivided attention. On that night, get out your honeymoon photos and reminisce. If you do not have pictures, share your memories. If you did not have a honeymoon, recall your first trip.

Chapter 4

BE SELFLESS

Lonnie Jones

*Selfishness is the most dangerous enemy
of man and marriage.*

G ranny Wallis was a strong, raw-boned woman who lived in Velvet
Ridge, Ark. Her husband, JT, had farmed the land, raising children,
cattle and strawberries. I was in love with their granddaughter. We stood
behind the old home place. I thought Granny was sweating (surely this
tough old woman wasn't crying) when she looked up from hoeing in
the garden spot with moisture running down her face and bluntly asked,
"You're planning on taking Jacque Lynn away, aren't you?"

I planned to marry her. That was true. I planned to create a life
with her. I planned on having her be part of my "grand adventure."
I'd never thought about it as "taking her away." But I was. That was
my plan. She was going to leave her childhood home, the friends of
her younger years, her parents, Granny and even her last name – and
I was going to ask her to do all that and "accomp'ny me," as Bob
Seger sang in my favorite song back then.

She was leaving them to be with me. Why on earth would she do
that? Suddenly, "because we were in love" didn't seem like enough
to me. That's when I seriously thought about what it was to be a
man, at least the kind of man that a woman should leave everything
and follow. If she were going to go away with me, to follow me on
this "grand adventure," I had to be someone she could trust. I had to

be worthy of that trust. I didn't know that at the time. I used other words. I had practiced a script from Jim Woodroof's "relationship language" and the Beatitudes.

Years later (27 to be exact) I was asked to write on the subject of being a better husband and to make a pledge to become the best husband ever. As I started on this path, my agenda for what I would write and become changed drastically.

How Do You Measure Trust?

My business – counseling, consulting and training – has made trust an area of expertise. I've taught the value of trust to church groups, clubs, teams and corporations. I've observed trust and the breach of trust. I've spent 20-plus years attached in an advisory role with a SWAT team and seen trust in life and death situations played out. I've watched men make hard entries into buildings with live weapons against hostile gunmen relying on each other for safety. I've climbed from the New River Gorge to Yosemite and placed my trust in climbing guides and a climbing partner.

I've walked the path of unconditional trust but never, ever tried to measure it. How do you gauge trust? How do you quantify trust? Read the *Rational Game Theory* as applied to the cold war think tanks. Research John Gottman's work *The Science of Trust* and his "trust metric," and you'll find one pivotal concept in trust. That concept boils down to this question: "Do you believe that this other person makes decisions based on your best interest or his?" If you believe that I make my decisions based on your interests rather than my own, then you trust me. If you don't hold that belief, you don't trust me. Simple as that.

It all began to dawn on me several summers ago. Coca-Cola was starting a signature program for youth just north of Atlanta. Camp Coca-Cola was to be for Coke what the Ronald McDonald Houses were for McDonald's. They chose children from Atlanta based on grades, leadership, teacher recommendation, and even letters from ministers, and hosted them at a Girl Scout camp in north Georgia. In the pilot program for Georgia, I was honored to be involved in running the challenge course or ropes course portion of the camp.

You Can Count on Me

One beautiful summer day in Georgia, I was working with middle school students on a trust fall. It is as advertised. One participant stands on an elevated platform and falls back into the arms of his "trusted" team. We take several precautions to avoid incidents, and one of the fundamental rules is that the faller keeps his or her hands tucked into a tight position while falling back. When you do a trust fall, there is a point that once the falling action is initiated you can't stop the ride. You are going to fall.

There is also a brief second where many people get that gut-dropping sensation and feel as if they've fallen too far and aren't going to be caught. A group of executives was touring the camp just as we were doing our exercise. The faller had that gut-level fear and swung his arms out to catch himself, shattering some glasses and breaking the nose of a little kid. This of course got the attention of the suits from the corporate office.

As we stood processing what had gone wrong, I finally asked the bleeding kid, "When he swung his arm at your face why didn't you move?" His answer forever changed my approach to the trust fall. He simply said, "I made a promise to catch him when he fell, and it didn't matter what he did. I promised to be there." Trust-fall debriefings are no longer about "Do you trust people enough to fall into their arms?" but rather "Can you be trusted to keep your promise?"

Ask a group of at-risk kids or even slightly dysfunctional adults this question: "During a trust fall, what made you more nervous, falling or catching someone?" The at-risk participants always answer that they are more scared falling. (Will you catch me? Will you fail me? Will you abandon me?) The leadership groups, successful sports teams, and even the happy couples always answer that they are more afraid when catching someone – the burden to be trustworthy. "I don't want to let you down" is more important to them. They are not thinking of self but thinking of others.

So the trust measure boils down to a fundamental belief as to the amount of selflessness or selfishness I bring to the relationship. To be the best husband ever, I must be selfless, putting her needs above my own.

How I See Myself

Philippians 2:3-8 lays out the groundwork for becoming this selfless man. The process is as follows: Do not do anything out of "selfish ambition or conceit, but in lowliness of mind let each esteem others better than himself." This is fundamentally a self-awareness check. How much of self controls my decisions? How much of self controls my actions toward others? Selfishness is the most dangerous enemy of man and marriage.

Selfishness is the common denominator to all sin. That is why all sin can be viewed as equal. There is no such thing as a "big" sin or a "little" sin. All sin is the manifestation of selfishness. Sin is a result of temptation, and those temptations are a result of our wants and sinful desires (James 1:13-15). Where self-seeking exists "every evil thing" is there (3:16).

Selfishness is opposite to Christianity. Jesus said, "If anyone desires to come after Me, let him deny himself, and take up his cross, and follow Me" (Matthew 16:24). You can't carry a cross and carry yourself. In measuring spiritual maturity, we find self-control listed in the characteristics that the Spirit produces (Galatians 5:22-23). Among love, joy, peace, longsuffering (patience), kindness, goodness, faithfulness and gentleness, we find the foundation of those things to be self-control. Selfishness is the opposite of love. I know that hate is the antonym of love, but selfishness is the antithesis of love.

Second, we must mitigate the value we place on ourselves. The New International Version doesn't just have "conceit" but "vain conceit" (Philippians 2:3). In other words, we are placing an inflated price tag on ourselves. That reminds me of the old phrase, "I'd like to buy him for what he's worth and sell him for what he thinks he's worth." In a relationship, we must change the value or importance we put on ourselves. We cannot expect to meet the needs of our spouses properly if we can't step away from our positions of importance and grandeur and see ourselves not as kings but as servants.

This transition of thought can come about only by a cognitive shift. "In lowliness of mind" (Philippians 2:3) is a thought process that has to take place in executing our plan to be the best husbands we can be. It is not about what my spouse does or does not do but only about what I promised to be. Remember what the kid with the bleeding nose said earlier? "I made a promise to catch him when he fell, and it didn't matter what he did. I promised to be there."

How I See Others

Viewing others differently can be accomplished only after getting "self" in the proper perspective. When Jesus told us that the second greatest command was to "love your neighbor as yourself" (Matthew 22:39), He was giving us instruction about viewing others from a proper perspective of self.

If I view myself as too grand or am narcissistic, then I can't see you as important or as special as I am. I have to worship you or totally discount you because of my delusions of grandeur. If I view myself as nothing, a thing with no value, then I can't treat you as valuable. The healthy self-concept – nothing done through selfish ambition or vain conceit (Philippians 2:3) – allows me to take a view that your needs can come first. I can put your needs above my wants or rights and treat you as the more important person. Thus in lowliness of mind, a humility of attitude, if you will, I can esteem others better than myself.

The result? "Let each of you look out not only for his own interests, but also for the interests of others." That verse from Philippians 2:4 is almost a direct quotation from the measure of trust that Gottman used in his book. Learning to be selfless and trustworthy seems to be inextricably linked. When we vowed to love our wives as Christ loved the church, we promised to be selfless. In promising to be selfless, we were making a commitment to put her needs above our rights and change the way we saw ourselves and the way we would forever see her.

HONEY-DO LIST: Item #4

Die to Self to Start Living

1. How would your wife rank you as a "selfless" husband?

   Circle a Number   1 2 3 4 5 6 7 8 9 10 +

2. Why not a lower number?

3. Name three things you could do this week to rank higher in her mind.

4. Which one would most make her feel treasured?

5. How could you go about making this change?

6. What would be the first step?

7. When and where could you begin this week? Be specific. Time? Place?

8. How committed are you to making this change to bring her more joy?

   Circle a Number   1 2 3 4 5 6 7 8 9 10 +

9. If your commitment level is less than a 9, go back to step 3 and be more creative.

Powering Up

Pray for God's help in becoming a Christlike husband by becoming more selfless. "Ask, and it will be given to you" (Matthew 7:7).

Marriage Magic

Find a night this week to have an hour of your wife's undivided attention. On that night, get out your wedding photos and reminisce together. What are her favorite memories? What can you learn about her from this experience? How can you use this information in the future?

Chapter 5

BE HELPFUL
Ben Hayes

What would our families be like
if we took up the towel?

As I write this chapter, I am completely aware of my shortcomings, not just in this area but in many others. As a minister, counselor, student and father of four, I am spread thin. My wife, a stay-at-home mother, bears the brunt of the work around the house. From daylight until dark I see her folding clothes, washing dishes, preparing food, giving baths, folding clothes, cleaning the house, working in the yard, playing with kids and folding more clothes. She is simply amazing. I am simply not. So as I write a chapter on being helpful, I am stepping on my own toes.

If I had to guess, many of you have wives just as spectacular. You have wives who work hard. You have wives who love you and support you and the rest of your family. When God created the woman from the rib of Adam, He was making a helper for Adam (Genesis 2:18, 22). However, there is no doubt in my mind that God intended for that relationship to be mutual. What is unfortunate is that much of what I see in today's world seems to stand in opposition to that idea. Even within our churches I see women who carry more than their share of the weight in the home, both in physical terms and the spiritual nourishment of the family.

For many years, the secular world and even our churches encouraged a world in which women had become practically slaves to the man. Even in homes where the woman worked a secular job outside the home, there was still the "Honey, I'm home" syndrome. The man came home and expected a nice warm meal on the table when he arrived, kids that would quietly leave him alone while he kicked back in a recliner after supper to vegetate while his wife waited on him hand and foot. One of two things happened in those scenarios: An angry wife or an angry husband. It is unlikely that things happened in that way, day in and day out, without that attitude becoming an issue to one or both of them very quickly.

A cartoon I recently read illustrates this well: "I've been thinking. I'm the man of this house, so starting tomorrow I want you to have a hot, delicious meal ready for me the second I walk through the door. Afterward, while watching ESPN and relaxing in my chair, you'll bring me my slippers and then run my bath. When I'm done with my bath, guess who's going to dress me and comb my hair?" The wife's reply was simple: "The funeral director." As I said, it is unlikely both man and woman will be equally fulfilled in such a relationship.

Let me relate a story of a different suppertime. This time the husband was a powerful son of a king. The family of this prince was unimpressive, selfish and at times difficult to deal with. On that night, he found himself taking on the role of a servant. He knew some would resist. He knew some would not appreciate His act. In fact, He knew one already had a plot against Him. At the same time, the young prince was also keenly aware of His own power. He was well aware of where He had come from and what His end would be. Knowing all these things, He "rose from supper and laid aside His garments; took a towel and girded Himself. After that, He poured water into a basin and began to wash the disciples' feet, and to wipe them with the towel with which He was girded" (John 13:4-5).

What a beautiful act of service! Jesus did not have to serve them that night. In fact, it could be argued that of all the people at that table He was the least deserving of such a task. The same argument could be used for His death on the cross. But the fact remains: Jesus served them and did so willingly. During another time together, Jesus had informed His disciples that His mission in life was not to be served, but to serve (Matthew 20:28). It wasn't just His day job to serve. It was His life. It was at His core.

Unfortunately, the idea of service today is not the most popular. Many people in organizations wage war for the top spot. Those spots are defended. Very rarely is service believed to be important. One look at Jesus and His leadership skills and our minds should be changed. Jesus did not have to fight for the top spot. Jesus did not mark off the duties of the group as too lowly or as being someone else's job. As C. Gene Wilkes wrote in his book *Jesus on Leadership*, "But Jesus showed us that leaders with towels are willing to meet whatever need exists – regardless of whose job it is."

What would our families be like if we took up the towel? What would it be like if as the husband, the man of the house, we took on the persona of Christ and served? What if we were helpful? How would the script of our marriage be altered? I would dare say that if a husband who is not doing so already, started helping and serving his wife that it would make a huge difference in their relationship.

I have often related to my clients that relationships are much like chemical combinations. You cannot remove one component without changing the whole thing. I don't think it is coincidence that we often refer to the connection between two people as "chemistry." For instance, if a couple has always argued and both participated, what happens when one refuses to argue? It changes the dynamic. Maybe for good and maybe not, but it can't help but be changed. Therefore, when the husband changes his way of doing things, it cannot help altering what is happening in the relationship. It might be a drastic difference or ever so slight, but it will change.

That makes sense when you think about what Jesus did in coming to earth. He flipped the script. He changed the view of God. The Father had been seemingly unapproachable. Now, in the Christian age, it is different. "And the Word became flesh, and dwelt among us, and we beheld His glory, the glory as of the only begotten of the Father, full of grace and truth" (John 1:14). In another passage John says, "That which was from the beginning, which we have heard, which we have seen with our eyes, which we have looked upon, and our hands have handled, concerning the Word of Life" (1 John 1:1). Jesus' coming forever changed the relationship between God and man. Especially because He approached that coming with the same kind of attitude with which I would encourage man to approach his wife.

One of my favorite passages is found in Philippians 2:5. Paul encourages his readers to have the same attitude as Jesus. The attitude that Paul explained in the following verses describe well the towel-wearing Prince we see in John 13. What qualities do we see? What attitude is apparent?

Make my joy complete by being of the same mind, maintaining the same love, united in spirit, intent on one purpose. Do
nothing from selfishness or empty conceit, but with humility
of mind regard one another as more important than yourselves;
do not merely look out for your own personal interests, but
also for the interests of others. (Philippians 2:2-4)

Entitlement

One of the hardest concepts to grasp in life is that it is not all about
us. In our current culture, we grow up with a selfish attitude. Slogans
for restaurants insist that we have it our way. Our kids grow up idolizing
performers and athletes who have it all and expect to be waited on hand
and foot. Entitlement is rampant in our society, and we seemingly feed
it more and more each day. Don't believe me? Go interview people who
worked in schools 40 years ago and those who work in schools today.
Once upon a time the adult was trusted and the parents and teachers
would work together. Now, parents march down to the school to defend
their children when they get in trouble. Many raise their children to never
take responsibility for their actions. Blame is placed on the teachers.

This may seem as though it doesn't apply to the topic at hand, but I
believe it does. You see, entitlement is the opposite of the attitude Christ
had. Entitlement says, "You owe it to me." Humility and looking out for
those around us says, "I owe it to you." Helping begins with a mindset,
and the problem is that our society continues to program children to expect
handouts from others and not to serve. That filters into our relationships.

Humility

Looking out for the people around you, specifically your wife and
family, begins with a mindset of humility. When Paul goes on to describe
that "attitude" of Christ (Philippians 2:5), he speaks of the things Jesus
gave up and the suffering He faced. Jesus had exited the throne room of
the King to enter the dirty, sinful streets of mankind. The Prince became
a pauper. "The Son of Man has nowhere to lay His head" (Luke 9:58).
The first step toward being a helping husband is stepping down from
the throne of greatness to see the needs of the family. When husbands

were encouraged to love their wives in Ephesians 5, the love was compared to the way Jesus "also loved the church and gave Himself for her" (v. 25). Why would a man who would give his life for his wife and children not also sacrifice his time and energy for them?

Jesus had a mindset of humility that fostered unity. Jesus was one with His followers, His bride. The idea of becoming one in marriage is foundational. Jesus stated:

> Have you not read that He who made them at the beginning "made them male and female," and said, "For this reason a man shall leave his father and mother and be joined to his wife, and the two shall become one flesh"? So then, they are no longer two but one flesh. Therefore what God has joined together, let not man separate. (Matthew 19:4-6)

God intended for man and wife to be joined in body and soul. I can't help thinking how strong a relationship between a husband and wife would be if the statement in Philippians 2:3-4 was a description of that bond. Many books have been written on the necessity of meeting each other's needs. Obviously the church should be a place where needs are met, but so should the home.

You want to impress your wife? Ask her how you can help and then do what she asks. Want to knock her socks off? Do something around the house without asking and do it without expecting something in return. When you sacrifice and put forth effort to help, it gets noticed. It may be a thankless job at times, but it gets noticed. If you get discouraged about how many times she doesn't say, "Thank you," then it might do well to think about how many times you said, "Thank you," when she did the same task.

The greatest man and bridegroom who ever lived spent a lifetime serving. He served people who were hurting by healing. He served people who were lost by showing them the way. He served people who were ignorant by teaching. He served the people who were closest to Him by doing the lowliest job He could think of – He washed their feet. When He explained Himself to them, these were His words: "I have given you an example, that you should do as I have done to you" (John 13:15). Let's follow in the footsteps of the bridegroom. Let's be helpful.

HONEY-DO LIST: Item #5
Make Helpfulness a Habit

1. How would your wife rank you as a "helpful" husband?

   Circle a Number   1 2 3 4 5 6 7 8 9 10 +

2. Why not a lower number?

3. Name three things you could do this week to rank higher in her mind.

4. Which one would most make her feel treasured?

5. How could you go about making this change?

6. What would be the first step?

7. When and where could you begin this week? Be specific. Time? Place?

8. How committed are you to making this change to bring her more joy?

   Circle a Number   1 2 3 4 5 6 7 8 9 10 +

9. If your commitment level is less than a 9, go back to step 3 and be more creative.

Powering Up

Pray for God's help in becoming a Christlike husband by becoming more helpful. "Seek, and you will find" (Matthew 7:7).

Marriage Magic

Arrange some uninterrupted time with your wife and reminisce about the day you proposed to her. What were you feeling when you asked her to marry you? What was she feeling when she said yes? What were your hopes and dreams at that moment?

Chapter 6

BE GRACIOUS

Cecil May Jr.

The kindest word of all
is the unkind word never said.

G raciousness is an attribute of God. Christians are told that "the Lord is gracious" (1 Peter 2:3). Newer translations, including the English Standard Version, render the phrase, "the Lord is good." Other synonyms of "gracious" include "kind," "courteous" and "forgiving."

The word describes God's kindness in extending grace to repentant sinners. Paul thought God's graciousness was being misunderstood by the Jews who were rejecting the gospel of Christ: "Or do you presume on the riches of his kindness and forbearance and patience, not knowing that God's kindness is meant to lead you to repentance?" (Romans 2:4 ESV). "Courtesy" is also included in graciousness. Good manners are the socially acceptable ways of being thoughtful of others. Because God is gracious to us, graciousness also reminds us of the need to forgive one another: "Be kind to one another, tenderhearted, forgiving one another, even as God in Christ forgave you" (Ephesians 4:32). So I understand "gracious" to mean: be kind, courteous and forgiving.

It is, of course, appropriate for the best husband ever to exhibit attributes of God; for God is the "husband" of His people in both the Old and New Testaments (Jeremiah 31:32; Ephesians 5:25).

Be Kind

A little girl was being prompted by her mother as she said her bed-time prayers. She prayed, as she did every night, "Bless Mama, bless Daddy, bless Grandmother, bless Uncle Mack and Aunt Irene." She paused for a moment and Mother prompted, "And bless all the bad people and help them to be good," so the little girl dutifully repeated, "And bless all the bad people and help them to be good." But then the little girl added, "And, God, please help all the good people to be nice." A distinction I suspect we all can appreciate. "Nice" to her, no doubt, meant kind.

Loving our wives as Christ loved the church requires being kind to them. Love is kind (1 Corinthians 13:4). Kindness massages sore necks, relieves overloaded hands and comforts sad hearts. If there is a need to correct a mistake she made, kindness does so privately. Our tone of voice should communicate love, gentleness and humility (Galatians 6:1). The kindest word of all is the unkind word never said.

Being kind to our wives means bearing some of their load. One wife expressed her joy at her husband's initiative in handling the garbage. She said she did not have to ask, much less beg. He did not demand or expect a "thank you." He simply accepted the fact that garbage was his job, and he took complete charge of it, very kindly relieving her of even having to think about it. What household task have we kindly assumed as our own?

Ralph Waldo Emerson famously said, "You cannot do a kindness too soon, for you never know how soon it will be too late."

Be Courteous

Most of us are probably courteous to people we meet without even having to think about it, even to strangers we never expect to see again. As well we should be. However, while being normally courteous to all, it is easy to forget to show common courtesy to the one we live with, the one, by the way, on whose contentment and happiness our own happiness primarily depends.

Courtesy requires that we not interrupt when we should be listening; that we open the door and stand back to let our wives go first. Courtesy requires a "please" to go with each request and a "thank you" in response to every favor. Being courteous means not taking the best piece of chicken or the last piece of cake. Much of courtesy is the same as simply not being selfish, taking care of her needs before we concern ourselves with our own.

Courtesy requires that we let our wives know where we are going and when we expect to be back home. When courting, we went to the passenger side of the car to open and hold the door for our date to get in. Should we be less courteous to our date now that she is our wife? Courtesy (graciousness) also rules out harsh rebukes and insulting epithets. "Let your speech always be with grace, seasoned with salt, that you may know how you ought to answer each one" (Colossians 4:6). The great love chapter of the Bible reminds us, love "does not behave rudely" (1 Corinthians 13:5).

Be Forgiving

"Be kind to one another, tenderhearted, forgiving one another, even as God in Christ forgave you" (Ephesians 4:32). Question: When two people who love each other have a disagreement that deteriorates into angry words or harsh and hasty actions, which one should apologize first?

There is a tendency for us to think, "Whichever is guilty," and, of course in our minds, it's not us. However, a better answer is, "Whichever is the more mature and stronger spiritually." Rarely in husband-wife disputes is either guilt or innocence one-sided. More importantly, guilt or innocence is not the most important issue.

We are to forgive "as God in Christ forgave" (Ephesians 4:32). Christ was still on the cross and His murderers and tormentors were at the height of their nefarious ridicule and torture when He cried, "Father, forgive them, for they do not know what they do" (Luke 23:34). Ideally, both husband and wife should work to cultivate a loving, Christlike, forgiving spirit. When the most important issue is maintaining or healing the relationship, the more mature spiritually one will take the initiative and apologize.

Forgiving is an outgrowth of loving as Christ loved. "Love is not resentful. Love bears all things … endures all things" (1 Corinthians 13:4, 7 ESV).

The difference between the sacrificial system of the Old Testament and that of the New is summed up in this contrast: Under the Old Testament, "in these sacrifices there is a reminder of sins every year" (Hebrews 10:3). Under the New, "Their sins and their lawless deeds I will remember no more" (v. 17). That should be a pattern for a husband to follow if his wife does or says something that offends him.

To refuse to forgive is to guarantee a troubled relationship. To say we forgive but to verbally recall it whenever some other disagreement arises means we have not truly forgiven. To say we forgive and forget does not necessarily mean it is completely gone from our memory; that may be beyond our ability to accomplish. It rather means we will not bring it up again and will not nurture it as a sore spot in our relationship.

Clara Barton, famous nurse and founder of the American Red Cross, refused to bear grudges. She was reminded by a friend of a wrong done to her some years earlier. "Don't you remember?" asked her friend. "No," replied Clara firmly. "I distinctly remember forgetting that." When we think our wives have done us wrong, we need to deliberately put it out of our mind. That especially means not bringing it back up if or when another offense occurs. A husband is never more Christlike than when he is kind, courteous and forgiving.

HONEY-DO LIST: Item #6

Give Her Grace, Not Grief

1. How would your wife rank you as a "gracious" husband?

   Circle a Number   1 2 3 4 5 6 7 8 9 10 +

2. Why not a lower number?

3. Name three things you could do this week to rank higher in her mind.

4. Which one would most make her feel treasured?

5. How could you go about making this change?

6. What would be the first step?

7. When and where could you begin this week? Be specific. Time? Place?

8. How committed are you to making this change to bring her more joy?

   Circle a Number   1 2 3 4 5 6 7 8 9 10 +

9. If your commitment level is less than a 9, go back to step 3 and be more creative.

Powering Up

Pray for God's help in becoming a Christlike husband by becoming more gracious. Knock and the door shall be opened unto you (Matthew 7:7). Of course, you may have to knock more than once.

Marriage Magic

Plan an unhurried evening with your wife when you both can be completely present. Share your memories about your first date. Where were you when you had your first kiss. What are some of your favorite dating memories? When did you first know you were in love? Can you recall when you first said, "I love you"?

Chapter 7

BE SACRIFICIAL
Lonnie Jones

Submission is not about giving up or giving in.
It is simply about giving.

As a kid watching Saturday night wrestling out of Atlanta, Ga., I was a big fan of any wrestler whose signature finishing move was a submission move. Colorful descriptors such as the figure-four leg lock, the Las Vegas leg lock, the Indian death lock, or the Scorpion come to mind. As a kid practicing Saturday night wrestling moves in the back yard with my brother and friends, it was a matter of pride to not ever submit if one found himself in the clutches of these tortures.

Years later as a pseudo-practitioner of various forms of jiujitsu, I've discovered it's no big deal to submit or tap out. It's just part of the sport, and if you do it long enough, someone, somewhere will make you tap. I have seen a T-shirt or two touting the sentiment "Real Men Don't Tap," and it's a lie. Only fools don't tap. Refusal to do so gets you put to sleep or gets something torn, popped or dislocated.

I'm not sure where we get the idea in our relationships that being the head of the wife, the spiritual leader or a real man means that we never submit. Only a fool doesn't submit. Only a person who is dead set on distance rather than intimacy doesn't submit. Only a person who doesn't understand the nature of Christianity refuses to submit. In fact, in order to be the best husband we can be we need to learn the nature of submission.

The Source of Significance

Submission in a marriage is a dual responsibility (not a duel) of both the husband and the wife, although many people think that submission is reserved solely for the women. Note that 1 Peter 3:1 says, "Wives, likewise, be submissive to your own husbands"; the likewise ties back to the instructions in verses 13-25 and has some strong inferences about the Christian being expected to "suffer for doing good" (v. 17). It is of note that verse 7 says, "husbands, likewise" or in the same way – letting men know that submission is one of our roles just as much as it is for women.

In the same way that service involves changing the way we see ourselves and the way we see others, submission also involves a shift in our point of view about ourselves and others. This shift in perspective is not just about value as in Philippians 2 but more of an awareness of a triangulated relationship. Ephesians 5:22–6:9 discusses the submission roles of husbands to wives, wives to husbands, parents to children, children to parents, slaves to masters, and masters to slaves. All those verses are held together by the bond of this antecedent attitude found in 5:21, "submitting to one another in the fear of God."

Being a submissive husband involves being a submissive Christian. I balance my relationship with my wife using my relationship with Christ as an orienting point on my compass. When I understand my responsibility and my response to Christ, I now have proper perspective for all my relationships.

The "Master" Plan

I am connected to Christ. How would Christ treat His bride? How would Christ treat your bride? How should I treat any person in my life who is also connected to Christ? How much more reverence, honor and submission should I grant a person who is connected to Christ, connected to me in the body, and is also one in the body with me?

The parameters for submission then start with an understanding that this isn't about my wife and me but more about me and my Master. Admitting we have a master implies submission. Because of my reverence for Christ, I have reverence for His body. My Christian wife is a member of that body and should be accorded that respect, honor and glory. I must love my wife "as Christ also loved the church and gave Himself for her" (Ephesians 5:25). He submitted to the needs of the church.

So how do we submit? First and foremost, we change the way we see ourselves. Second, we change the way we see our wives. My wife is connected to Christ, and as a part of Christ my behavior toward her is balanced by my relationship or connection to Christ.

Connected Through Christ

My daughter has a young man in her life. My wife and I have spent limited time with him. He's very different from me. He's a business major with a master's degree in education. He paid for college by playing basketball. He's a fisherman and a golfer. He is not a fan of heights. He does not shoot or hunt. We've never wrestled. Yet he is very special to me. It has nothing to do with his likes, interests or personality. We are connected through Loni Beth. Because she loves him, we love him. Because she welcomes him, we welcome him. Because he is special to her, he is special to us. His connection to me is because and through our mutual connection to Loni Beth.

If the whole in-law thing is hard to wrap your mind around, then try the grandparent thing. If you are a grandparent, you love your children's children. They are not your children, but because they are connected to you by your children you love and adore them. In fact most of us act downright "twitter pated" when it comes to these little people. Their value is not inherent. It is conferred on them because of a shared connection.

My bride is a member of Christ's bride. She is special to God and therefore, by default and without reservation or hesitation, she is very special to me. I therefore submit to her well-being because I am submissive to the one she is connected to and we are connected through.

Submit to one another because of your mutual connection to Christ. So what are the practical steps to making this happen? Submission can be exemplified by these actions in Ephesians 5:22-30.

(1) Love your wife as Christ loved the church (Ephesians 5:25). This is sacrificial giving. This is the abdication of self. This is elevating her

to the position of prominence. This is putting her needs above your rights. That means protecting her at your own expense.

(2) Give yourself for your wife (Ephesians 5:26-27). Christ's purpose was to act in such a way that His bride was presentable to God or to Himself without spot, stain, wrinkle or blemish. He acted in such a way as to wash, cleanse and sanctify her. What did that cost Him? Everything. He was stained, blemished, beaten and bruised in order to create or preserve this pristine condition of His bride. Eliminate selfishness and give yourself for and to your wife.

(3) Love your wife as your own body (Ephesians 5:28-30). On some level we may not get the whole selfless concept. We are after all humans and male humans at that. We tend to be egocentric. We have a natural pull toward self and self-gratification. Jesus covered this in a simple rule that we call "golden" or James describes as the royal law. Think in terms of yourself and then treat others like you would want to be treated. Simply put, I should consider my behavior, thoughts and words as if I were the one receiving them. If I don't like them in that context, then don't say them or do them.

The whole concept of "nourish" and "cherish" your wife with the same love you would want for yourself is what is covered here.

More Than Puppy Love

Probably not the best example in a husband book, but I watched an amazing transformation in the life of my daughter. We ended up with a Yorkie named Max. Loni Beth fell in love with him, and so did Jacque. When Loni Beth moved to Rome, Ga., Max stayed in Gurley, Ala., with us.

As time went on, we found Max a girlfriend, and they produced a litter of puppies, one of which is Bentley. He belongs to Loni Beth. Our daughter is a wonderful child, but she is an only child and for nearly 15 years was the only grandchild in either of our parents' lives. So she is naturally a little "me" oriented.

Suddenly with Bentley, there was a transformation. She spent her money on Bentley. She's cleaned up his puddles. She'd watch for his safety with paranoid diligence. While she was in high school, I'd put on my body armor and take a long stick to wake her up in the mornings.

Now she gets up cheerfully in the night and early in the morning to let him outside or take care of his needs. It's a strange combination of a little girl playing with a live doll and a young woman learning to be sacrificial and nourishing, putting the needs of this little love of hers before her own conveniences.

Bentley is nourished and cherished. Loni Beth leaves work on her lunch break to go across town to take him out. She frets if she thinks he is not getting enough attention or interaction. She spends money she can't afford to address any medical issues with the vet. Nourish: provide all the needs. Cherish: to treat as special, and in a relationship as the most special – even beyond self.

Submission is not about relinquishing power to someone. It is not about giving up or giving in. Submission is simply about giving.

HONEY-DO LIST: Item #7

Make a Daily Sacrifice for Her

1. How would your wife rank you as a "sacrificial" husband?

   Circle a Number   1 2 3 4 5 6 7 8 9 10 +

2. Why not a lower number?

3. Name three things you could do this week to rank higher in her mind.

4. Which one would most make her feel treasured?

5. How could you go about making this change?

6. What would be the first step?

7. When and where could you begin this week? Be specific. Time? Place?

8. How committed are you to making this change to bring her more joy?

   Circle a Number   1 2 3 4 5 6 7 8 9 10 +

9. If your commitment level is less than a 9, go back to step 3 and be more creative.

Powering Up

Ask God to help you put your wife's needs above any other desire of your heart. Rejoice in the opportunity to make sacrifices that will relieve her burdens or gladden her heart.

Marriage Magic

Ask your wife to choose a household project she would like you to work on together. Set a time this week, and do not let lesser priorities interfere. It is not just about the project. It is about building a life together where you solve problems. Communication and cooperation take practice, and practice will prepare you for even bigger challenges ahead.

Chapter 8

BE FRIENDS
Ben Hayes

*In a world where half of marriages fail,
having a marriage built on the foundation of
friendship doesn't sound like such a bad idea.*

I cannot tell you how many times I have heard this line from a teenager: "I can't date him; he's my friend!" The older I get, the crazier that logic sounds. Don't get me wrong, I am not saying there is no need for physical attraction. I am also not implying that one should simply marry someone because they are friends, but I do believe friendship is a colossal part of marriage.

Friendships begin and end with a mutual respect for one another. Friends can typically weather difficult storms. As the Scripture says, "A friend loves at all times" (Proverbs 17:17). In fact, some of the first people we truly love are friends. I'm not talking about romantic love. I'm talking about the kind of love that takes a punch for a friend, spends late hours listening to problems, or simply enjoys a run to the closest place that sells ice cream or coffee.

Since when did being married mean the fun ended? Hollywood has for years tried to break down the idea of marriage. Many times marriage on television or on the big screen is portrayed as mind-numbingly boring or an overly frustrating existence. Unfortunately, many families have indeed fallen into these two situations. We get so tied up being parents to our busy children or caretakers to our aging parents that we neglect the work of forging a strong friendship with each other.

Hearts Adrift

Most of the time when couples have "drifted apart" it is because they have put very little effort into spending time as friends. For many of us the dating experience involved talking in a restaurant for hours, walking in the park, hanging out in coffee shops, or sitting on a couch talking about all the things we enjoy. Each person would listen intently because he or she cared about the person speaking. After marriage, many people get caught up in the responsibilities and pressures of life. Consequently, those things that helped to build the relationship begin to be neglected. At this point, husbands and wives begin to wonder where the fire in their marriage has gone.

Unfortunately, some people today skip this part of the dating relationship altogether and are simply building upon a more physical relationship. Modern media encourage sexual activity early in relationships. The concept of waiting for the second date for a kiss sounds almost laughable to many people today. Much like our faith, relationships will stand or fall based on the foundation of the relationship. Friendship and companionship make for a strong and secure foundation. Sex can be a great component of companionship, but it can never be the foundation. That is why God wanted it reserved for marriage. It should be the reward for building strong relationships first.

In this study we are concerned about being the best husband ever. Although we cannot make our wives be our friends, we can work on being the best friend we can be to our wives. Although this might not always result in a mutual friendship between you and your spouse, when you consider the things women most desire in relationships, it is hard to believe it would not work the majority of the time.

Think Outside the Box

Willard F. Harley Jr., the best-selling author of *His Needs, Her Needs*, surveyed thousands of men and women and found that the top five needs of women were affection, conversation, honesty/openness, financial security and family commitment. Unfortunately, our needs as men are much different. Men desire sexual fulfillment, recreational companionship, an attractive spouse, domestic support and admiration. But what we typically seek for our fulfillment will not necessarily bring fulfillment for our spouses. Being a husband will require thinking and acting outside the box.

Jesus, the best husband ever, was good at thinking outside the box. Jesus lived outside the box. His thoughts, teachings and actions were far-removed from the majority of those living in His day. In fact, many of the things Jesus taught were so foreign to the way people thought at that time they began to persecute Him and His followers. Jesus was not only the bridegroom to the church but He was also a true friend.

Everything Jesus did on this earth served to prove His friendship to us. He said, "Greater love has no one than this, that one lay down his life for his friends. You are My friends if you do whatever I command you" (John 15:13-14). Jesus' friendship is not conditional. He has already sacrificed for us. We, on the other hand, have to choose to be His friend by committing to following Him. As Christian husbands, should we not also be concerned about proving our friendship to our wives? In the following pages, I will discuss three qualities that can build the friendship between you and your wife. They just so happen to be closely related to the top three needs of women discussed by Harley. Who knows? They could help you to become one of the best husbands ever.

No Quick Fix

Listen up, guys. No, really, listen. This is one of the hardest things for men to do. Communication is not our strong point. It is not as if we cannot talk. It is usually an issue because we have difficulty with the other end of communication – listening. Maybe it is just me, but I have to work overtime at it. Women seem better at it than men. In fact, it is probably why women would rather talk to their friends about problems than come to their husbands.

Men are usually fixers. We listen to our wives (or anybody for that matter) long enough to get the right amount of information to begin to develop a plan for resolving the issue. Not long into that cerebral process, we begin to tune out comments and begin developing a response.

If she gets lucky, she can finish her comment before being interrupted with the solution. Usually, she leaves the conversation frustrated, and we feel proud for having been the hero to her problems and do not understand why she just slammed the door on her way out.

Most men have learned that lesson the hard way. Hopefully you are beginning to develop a better plan for listening to your wife. Active listening is a concept that is talked about a lot in counseling circles. It is disciplining oneself to listen to the full comment and then to paraphrase the main idea back to the person who first said it. The point is twofold: they feel heard, and it serves to confirm that the message has been interpreted correctly. I have experienced many arguments over something that one of us thought the other said when they did not mean it that way at all. It just came out the wrong way. A little patience and paraphrasing might have saved you from another drawn-out fight.

Jesus is a great listener, isn't He? Peter tells us to cast "all your care upon Him, for He cares for you" (1 Peter 5:7). Peter had firsthand ministry experience at the feet of Jesus. He saw Him in action each day, and he knew that Jesus was the kind of person who listened and cared. He heard Jesus speak the words found in Matthew 11:28-30:

> Come to Me, all you who labor and are heavy laden, and I will give you rest. Take My yoke upon you and learn from Me, for I am gentle and lowly in heart, and you will find rest for your souls. For My yoke is easy and My burden is light.

I realize the words of Jesus in this passage are not specifically talking about communicating with Him, but they make you want to sit down and converse with Him. Do you provide that kind of safe environment for your spouse to talk to you?

Truth and Trust

Harley speaks of openness and honesty as one of the top needs of women. Honesty, in all relationships, really is the best policy. You have probably experienced that trust is hard to earn, especially if it has ever been broken. Jesus told His disciples on the night He was betrayed, "If it were not so, I would have told you" (John 14:2). Jesus' ministry was built on trust. These men had left everything to follow Him. They needed to know that what they were doing was worthwhile. They needed openness and honesty from their leader. They needed the truth.

Your wife, too, left her home and family. She chose you to be the one to whom she would become "one flesh." She deserves truthfulness in the relationship. There was a saying I used to hear more than I do now that went like this: "Friends don't make secrets, and secrets don't make friends." In a marriage that is 100 percent accurate. Keeping secrets usually requires deception or lies; neither of which build relationships.

When addressing the Christians in Ephesus, Paul wrote, "Putting away lying, 'Let each one of you speak truth with his neighbor,' for we are members of one another" (Ephesians 4:25). The reason Paul encouraged truth is because we are "members of one another." As Christian spouses, we have a double responsibility to honor the relationship and to speak truth. We are members of one another as brothers and sisters in Christ and as spouses.

Show and Tell

As I mentioned earlier in this chapter, sex is many times portrayed as the most important part of an intimate relationship between men and women. Various media outlets not only encourage it through movies, television and songs but have basically redefined what is normal in relationships. Most people would still consider me fairly young, yet I can remember when things on movies and mainstream television were not nearly as "liberal" as they are today. The problem is that while the sex craze feeds a man's needs (in an unhealthy way), it also fails to teach men accurately of the needs of women.

Harley says that the first need most women have is not sex but affection. He calls it "the cement of a relationship." Showing affection might not be the easiest thing in the world for you to do. It is not my greatest strength either. However, what would you be willing to do to make your marriage a success? Many of you would walk across the desert with no shoes or wrestle an alligator to keep a strong relationship with your spouse. I suppose some of you might think those scenarios sound like more fun than trying to show affection, but it is not nearly as difficult as it sounds.

You can have a lot of great qualities as a man, but without the ability to be affectionate, your wife is likely to feel unfulfilled in the relationship.

Affection can be displayed in a variety of ways: cards, flowers, hugs, invitations to dinner, opening a door, etc. Find a way to show and tell her how much you love her each day.

The Final Word

Some of these things may be difficult and might require something of a sacrifice for us. Sacrifice was the first quality of Christ. He left the throne room of God to travel to lowly Bethlehem as a baby only to find no room in the inn and very little room in the hearts of mankind during His time on the earth. Just as Jesus left home, a man is called to "leave his father and mother and be joined to his wife" (Genesis 2:24; Mark 10:7; Ephesians 5:31). Jesus sacrificed time and energy. His life was not about His wants and wishes. He lived for helping and building up others. Many people talk sacrifice, but few people live up to it. The best husband ever did both.

There are probably many other things that could help develop friendship within your marriage, but a good foundation can be provided through good communication, a dedication to truthfulness and displaying affection. If these qualities are present, it does not absolutely guarantee perfect marital bliss. However, without these qualities the relationship will certainly be lacking the strength that weathers storms. Friends love at all times (Proverbs 17:17) and love never fails (1 Corinthians 13:8). In a world where half of marriages fail, having a marriage built on the foundation of friendship doesn't sound like such a bad idea to me. I hope and pray that each of us can cultivate a friendship with our spouse that can hold strong through all the difficult days and stand the test of time.

HONEY-DO LIST: Item #8
Make Her My Best Friend

1. How would your wife rank you as a "friend"?

   Circle a Number   1 2 3 4 5 6 7 8 9 10 +

2. Why not a lower number?

3. Name three things you could do this week to rank higher in her mind.

4. Which one would most make her feel treasured?

5. How could you go about making this change?

6. What would be the first step?

7. When and where could you begin this week? Be specific. Time? Place?

8. How committed are you to making this change to bring her more joy?

   Circle a Number   1 2 3 4 5 6 7 8 9 10 +

9. If your commitment level is less than a 9, go back to step 3 and be more creative.

Powering Up

Pray for God's help in becoming a Christlike husband by becoming your wife's best friend. Remember, he who has friends must himself be friendly (Proverbs 18:24). Lead the way.

Marriage Magic

How well do you and your wife know each other? Write your answers to the lists on the next page on a separate piece of paper. Try to guess each other's response before the answer is revealed. Close couples delight in getting to know each other intimately. Knowing and being known are the essence of love.

MY FAVORITES

1. Singer _____
2. Song _____
3. Movie star _____
4. Movie _____
5. TV star _____
6. TV show _____
7. Author _____
8. Book _____
9. Magazine_____

10. Food _____
11. Dessert_____
12. Hobby _____
13. Bible book_____
14. Bible verse _____
15. Bible character _____
16. Worship song _____
17. Part of worship _____
18. Quality of my spouse
(not limited to one) _____

MY FEARS

1. Childhood fear _____
2. Adult fear _____

MY FUTURE

1. My dream for our marriage

_____

2. My dream for our family

_____

3. My dream for our finances

_____

4. My dream just for me

_____

Chapter 9

BE SUPPORTIVE
Cecil May Jr.

It is often said that "chivalry is dead,"
but it should not be.

S upposedly, someone speaking to the French Parliament remarked in passing, "Men are different from women." A member of the Parliament immediately stood and shouted, "*Vive la difference!*" Most readers of this book would concur with that sentiment, but there is a strong push among extreme feminists and political liberals to minimize the difference. God, however, in His act of creation, assigned different roles in the bearing of children and, in His Book, different roles for the genders in the home and in church assemblies.

God said, "It is not good that man should be alone." He made him a companion and helper exactly suited to his desires and needs (Genesis 2:18). Wisdom says, "He who finds a wife finds a good thing, and obtains favor from the LORD" (Proverbs 18:22). Christian husbands enthusiastically affirm that assessment. Man is appointed by God to be a leader in the home. It is appropriate, therefore, to say to husbands, "Be supportive." To be a good husband, most assuredly to be the best husband ever, we are to lovingly and cheerfully support our wives financially, verbally, emotionally and spiritually.

Be Supportive Financially

Not many things are said to be worse than not believing in Christ, except for a man to fail to provide for his family. In context the discussion has to do with adult children providing for their aged parents or grandparents, but the principle is stated broadly. "If anyone does not provide for his own, and especially for those of his household, he has denied the faith and is worse than an unbeliever" (1 Timothy 5:8).

Scripture supports what has been a traditional division of labor between husband and wife in the home; the husband is the provider, and the wife is the manager. Paul said, "I desire that the younger widows marry, bear children, manage the house, give no opportunity to the adversary to speak reproachfully" (1 Timothy 5:14). Although the discussion in this context concerns widows, the same charge is no doubt given to all who marry.

In the passage where the Scripture forbids women to exercise authority or leadership over men in prayer and Bible teaching (1 Timothy 2:8-15), the last thing said in that context is, "She will be saved in childbearing if they continue in faith, love, and holiness, with self-control" (v. 15). Unanimous agreement among writers and students regarding the meaning of those words is not to be found, but I understand the apostle to be saying that women's assigned sphere of influence, while not found in teaching or exercising authority over men, is rather to be found in the management of home and children. Traditionally, following this assignment of roles, men have been the breadwinner and women the homemaker.

These assigned roles have never been so absolute, however, that women could not participate in bringing in the paycheck or that men could not help manage the household. In another passage men are given a primary role in the rearing of children. "Fathers, do not provoke your children to wrath, but bring them up in the training and admonition of the Lord" (Ephesians 6:4). The "virtuous wife" in Proverbs 31 is described as an astute business woman contributing substantially to the family income. "She seeks wool and flax, and willingly works with her hands" (v. 13). "She considers a field and buys it; from her profits she plants a vineyard" (v. 16). "She perceives that her merchandise is good, and her lamp does not go out by night" (v. 18).

"Working mothers" is a redundant phrase, but the days when most mothers were "stay-at-home moms" are long gone. It more often than not takes two incomes for a family to survive in today's economy. When the wife contributes to providing family income, the supportive husband should help out proportionally with the housework. There are households headed by single moms or single dads because of circumstances over which they had no control. It is difficult for a woman to be a dad and also for a man to be a mom, but we commend and commit to God's grace those who are forced into this situation. Many do very well.

It is still true, however, that children are greatly blessed to be at home with a loving mother during preschool years and come home to a waiting and welcoming mother after school. No vocation is more honorable or rewarding than wife and mother. The benefits to family and children of a mother at home, especially while children are still small, far exceed the value of a second income if sought just for more trinkets, a more imposing house or bigger and more impressive automobiles. Blessed is the mother who fills that role, and blessed also is the supportive husband who makes it possible.

Be Supportive Verbally

Husbands who are controlling and verbally abusive violate a clear command of Scripture, "Husbands, love your wives, and do not be bitter toward them" (Colossians 3:19). Insults and demeaning epithets should never be spoken. Both angry shouting and silent pouting are tactics that have no place in a loving home. Supportive husbands will not employ them.

An annoying, hurtful tactic used too often by too many husbands is the public put-down, supposedly jokingly, of their wives. Many stinging truths are spoken as jests. Jokes that have a barb that attacks and catches the wife are out of order. "My wife was born a day late and has not caught up since." "My wife can't boil water without burning it." You may think of your own examples. Here is a rule for whether to make your wife the butt of a joke: unless what it suggests is so obviously not true that no one could possibly think you mean it, do not use it.

All of those examples approach what it means to be supportive from a negative standpoint. Avoid those negatives, but more importantly look for ways to be positively encouraging and complimentary. When she is dressed up and looks nice, tell her so. If she cooks a good meal or makes a delicious contribution to the church potluck, tell others what a great cook she is at a time and place when she can hear. If she does something that pleases you, tell her so and thank her. In addition to blessing our wives, speaking supporting words could be serendipitous; activities that are praised tend to be repeated.

When you talk to others about her and about your relationship with her, always do so in positive, complimentary terms. Look for opportunities to say things that put her in a positive light to your friends and acquaintances. When you have something to complain about, do it privately and meekly, considering yourself lest you also have done things she could legitimately complain about (see Galatians 6:1).

"I love you" can be said neither too fervently nor too often. If you have children at home they need to hear you compliment their mother and express your love to her. They, then, will know how to treat their spouses when they marry and will be helped to feel secure in a home they are confident will not be broken.

About the "virtuous wife" of Proverbs 31:10, the wise man said, "Her children rise up and call her blessed; her husband also, and he praises her" (v. 28). She deserves the praise. It may also be that the praise of her husband and children contribute to her excellence.

Be Supportive Emotionally

The writer asked, "Who can find a virtuous wife? Then after affirming that "her worth is far above rubies," the next thing he says is, "The heart of her husband safely trusts her" (Proverbs 31:10-11). An absolutely foundational element of marital love is trust. The husband must trust his wife, and the husband must give his wife every reason to trust him and no occasion to doubt his love or faithfulness.

Wisdom says:

> Drink water from your own cistern, and running water from your own well. Should your fountains be dispersed abroad, streams of water in the streets? Let them be only your own, and not for strangers with you. Let your fountain be blessed, and rejoice with the wife of your youth. As a loving deer and a graceful doe, let her breasts satisfy you at all times;

and always be enraptured with her love. For why should you, my son, be enraptured by an immoral woman, and be embraced in the arms of a seductress? For the ways of man are before the eyes of the LORD, and He ponders all his paths. (Proverbs 5:15-21)

In clear and pointed terms we are reminded of the dangers of flirting with sin, contrasted with the delights of love in a committed, loving relationship, free of guilt or fear. The Bible says, "Flee sexual immorality" (1 Corinthians 6:18). Joseph is a good example. When one first begins to feel a strong emotional bond with a woman other than his wife, it is time to sever the relationship. Office friendships, Facebook friends and other social connections should be carefully monitored. A clear warning sign is anytime you are thinking of doing something with someone, and you do not want your wife to know. Be open and transparent. Let your wife know your social media passwords. Share the same email account. Make it obvious you have nothing to hide. The "bottom line" of husband/wife relationships is, "Nevertheless let each one of you in particular so love his own wife as himself, and let the wife see that she respects her husband" (Ephesians 5:33). Respect is built on trust.

Peter commanded, "Husbands, likewise, dwell with them with understanding, giving honor to the wife, as to the weaker vessel, and as being heirs together of the grace of life, that your prayers may not be hindered" (1 Peter 3:7). Women are not "weaker" in every aspect. They usually live longer. They may be smarter. But they are generally weaker physically. The stronger male is to be aware of his strength and not ever use it to hurt her. He is to protect her from harm, even to the extent of giving his own life for hers, as Christ gave Himself for His church (Ephesians 5:25-29). While bravely considering himself to be his wife's protector against criminals, he should also remember he is the one in a position to hurt her the most and carefully guard his own words and actions.

It is often said that "chivalry is dead," but it should not be. Chivalry is a way for men to show "honor to the wife, as to the weaker vessel" (1 Peter 3:7). Hold doors for her to let her go in first. Open the car door for her. Quickly pick up things she drops, carry her heavy loads, open her jars and stand between her and danger. Extreme feminists may resent such chivalry, but Christian wives will appreciate and be grateful for it.

Be Supportive Spiritually

God appointed the husband and father as the head of the household for the purpose of spiritual leadership. In effect, man is God's deputy in the home. Abraham is our model. God said of him, "For I have known him, in order that he may command his children and his household after him, that they keep the way of the LORD, to do righteousness and justice" (Genesis 18:19).

Joshua also showed the way:

> Now therefore, fear the LORD, serve Him in sincerity and in truth, and put away the gods which your fathers served on the other side of the River and in Egypt. Serve the LORD! And if it seems evil to you to serve the LORD, choose for yourselves this day whom you will serve, whether the gods which your fathers served that were on the other side of the River, or the gods of the Amorites, in whose land you dwell. But as for me and my house, we will serve the LORD. (Joshua 24:14-15)

There may be a few exceptions, but if a man leads his house through biblical teaching and by his example to love and follow the Lord, the family will respect him and follow his lead.

Unfortunately, far too many men have abdicated their spiritual head-ship. If there is anyone to take the lead in getting the family ready for congregational Bible study and worship assemblies, it is more likely the wife and mother. If anyone has the spiritual perception and backbone to say, "You are not going out in public dressed like that!" it is too often the mother, not the dad. God bless the wives, mothers and even the children who have led the way to the Lord's church even when Dad lags behind. The best husband ever will be the one providing spiritual leadership for his family.

Some men think if their wife wants a dishwasher and they want a new set of golf clubs and they get the golf clubs, that action shows he is head of his house. Actually, it shows he is selfish and inconsiderate; it has nothing to do with the spiritual headship God established for men. Man up, dads and husbands! "Watch, stand fast in the faith, be brave, be strong" (1 Corinthians 16:13). Study your Bible diligently and regularly. Earnestly seek the will of the Lord. Base moral decisions on God's will; tell your family the biblical reasons for them. Show by your conversation that you respect Scripture as God's Word and intend to follow it – and that you expect your family to do the same. By precept and example lead your family to be faithful, sound and devout in service to the Lord.

Conclusion

Be a strong and cheerful supporter of your wife financially, verbally, emotionally and spiritually. Assure her continually of your love, your trust, your respect and your joy at being her husband. Work hard at being the best husband ever.

HONEY-DO LIST: Item #9
Give Her Support, Not Stress

1. How would your wife rank you as a "supportive" husband?

   Circle a Number   1 2 3 4 5 6 7 8 9 10 +

2. Why not a lower number?

3. Name three things you could do this week to rank higher in her mind.

4. Which one would most make her feel treasured?

5. How could you go about making this change?

6. What would be the first step?

7. When and where could you begin this week? Be specific. Time? Place?

8. How committed are you to making this change to bring her more joy?

   Circle a Number   1 2 3 4 5 6 7 8 9 10 +

9. If your commitment level is less than a 9, go back to step 3 and be more creative.

Powering Up

Pray for God's help in becoming a Christlike husband by becoming more supportive. People in love specialize in bearing one another's burdens (Galatians 6:2). Ask for strength to do this with grace.

Marriage Magic

Think of a couple that both you and your wife admire. Arrange to drop by their house or to invite them to your place. Ask each of them to share the secret of their successful marriage. What were the turning points? What have they learned along the way? What advice would they give you? Be sure to thank them for their advice and example.

Chapter 10

BE FORGIVING
Lonnie Jones

*Enter each day of your life
with no unfinished business.*

There are lots of "mantras" that have been prevalent in my life. Often stated in groups of three axioms, I have always thought of them as triads. My daughter was always told, "No harness, no helmet, no climbing." Or in self-defense there is "Space equals escape. Contact equals control. Control the head; control the body." In fighting (aka aggressive self-defense) there is "control the head, control the hips, and control the hands." At the end of any youth event that we were in charge of – retreat, rally, trip, etc. – we'd be walking out the door and many times I'd make eye contact with Derek Horst and one of us would say, "First one in." The other would say, "Last one out."

Years ago I heard Jim Baird speak at Leaders for Christ at Oklahoma Christian University, and his triad was "Submission, Service and Forgiveness." Anyone who is anyone in the kingdom has the ability to do those three things or possess those qualities. In thinking about being a better husband, I chose that triad as my model. We probably see submission and service as proactive and have a hard time putting forgiveness on our "to do" list because it seems to be passive or reactive. I have observed a lot of enduring vulnerabilities in people's psyche because of unhealed (unforgiven) wounds that create unfinished business and lead to resentment, contempt or withdrawal. To be the best husband I can be, I must be able to deal with the imperfections of the imperfect wife I married.

The Devil's Foothold

Maybe the first place to start is with the prohibition not to let the sun go down on your wrath from Ephesians 4:26. The flow of thought is to be angry and not sin. Don't let the day end with you still angry. Don't allow "the devil a foothold" (v. 27 NIV84). As much as I'd like this "foothold" to be a rock-climbing term, it is actually a military concept. This foothold would mean giving up ground in our hearts or minds and allowing the devil to conquer the territory of emotions or attitudes one piece at a time. Several years ago I wrote a small piece about not forgiving or holding a grudge.

> I am not really sure where it came from. Looking back, I think it probably snuck into the car while the trunk was open. Maybe it was in my coat when I grabbed it and stalked out that Sunday morning the preacher made me mad. No, no, it could have been in the baby's bag, and we left in such a hurry after the elders made the announcement about the nursery and crying babies. Actually, it could have come from just about anywhere. Maybe it got in my wallet when they announced the special contribution, and I closed it so fast. Maybe I brought it inside my Bible. It would have had time to grow undisturbed in there. You see I don't open my Bible at home because I'm so busy. I really can't tell where it came from.

> Nonetheless, I ended up carrying this little grudge home with me. It seemed pretty cute at the time. It made me feel special and important. That little grudge that I brought home with me only focused on my feelings. I didn't know at the time that the little grudge would eat so well. It fact, it was very easy to feed. It fed on the slightest things. Almost like it was just looking for something to keep it alive. It grew pretty fast too. In fact, I would end up missing services to stay home and tend to my grudge.

I never told anyone about my grudge. I just kept it, held it, nurtured it and fed it. After a few weeks, my grudge was so important to me that I just quit going altogether. There was nothing anyone could do. If someone came to see me, my grudge would feed on their "holier-than-thou" attitude. You see my grudge can see things that aren't even there. If no one came to see me, my grudge could digest that as isolation and neglect from them. I never thought that taking that little grudge home with me could turn into such a mess. By this time I no longer owned it, but it owned me. If I hadn't allowed it to feed or if I'd only exposed it to the light, it might have just gone away. As it is, I think it was fed so much and got so big that it had to molt. Once it got really hard and dead on the outside and sat there a few days, when it emerged from that hard shell, I think my little grudge had turned into resentment. Now the resentment at my house has cost me my soul, the soul of my wife and my little ones, and it all started when I carried home a little grudge.

The Unforgiving Man

There is no place in marriage for keeping, tending and nesting little grudges. Do not let wounds, actual or perceived, go unforgiven. Once we let them take residence in our lives, they ruin our ability to interpret our spouse's actions as anything but hurtful or negative.

Jesus told the story in Matthew 18 of a king who forgave the servant who owed him more money than he could repay in 150,000 years. This newly forgiven servant goes out and abuses another servant who was indebted to him for 18 years. Often we read this story and think the emphasis is that we should realize how great a debt we've been pardoned and thus should pardon the insignificant offenses of our brothers. My understanding is that although the debt he was owed was not as tremendous as the one he had been forgiven, it was still a major debt.

I can and should forgive insignificant slights; they don't matter in the long run. The point of this parable was that we are obligated to forgive the significant issues. Don't sweat the small stuff because it is small stuff. Unforgiven issues become footholds for the devil to take over our attitudes and ruin our lives and relationships.

A Recipe for Forgiveness

Forgiveness is achieved by the following recipe, if a recipe counts as things to remove as well as things to add.

- Remove bitterness, wrath, anger, clamor and evil speaking – and don't forget the malice (Ephesians 4:31).
- Once these are removed, add kindness, a tender heart and remember the story of the compassionate king. Forgive "as God in Christ forgave you" (Ephesians 4:32).

The function of forgiving the hurts and regrettable events of the past is to achieve a fresh start every day. We enter each new day of our lives with no unfinished business. When I end each day by asking God to forgive me and to forgive you, by being forgiving myself, I begin each new day as a new day. I'm not carrying over any wounds, hurts or grudges that affect my behavior toward my wife – or anyone else for that matter.

Write It Off

I own my own counseling practice where I provide services for a fee. Over the years I've done different billing practices. There have been those folks who have not paid their bills. At one time I could have told you who they were and what they owed.

I began to realize that on the day of the week or the month that I went through the books and tried to settle those accounts I'd get a bit frustrated. They had come in good faith, used my services, agreed to pay, actually been helped and had not paid me. It's not that I don't offer pro bono services to those who need it. Here I was being angry at people who had not paid for my time and literally giving them more of it to ruminate over an unpaid debt. Some of those debts were small, and some of them not so small.

Finally I learned to literally write it off. I don't have to keep up with what is "owed" me. Once I do, I am owned by what is owed. I have to make sure I don't have any outstanding debts – unfinished business – and if I take care of my "debts," that's all that really matters.

Matthew 5:23-24 says that as I approach God, I do not come into His presence thinking about what I am owed but rather considering whether my brother has something against me. If that is the case, I should leave what I am bringing to God and go reconcile with my brother. How sad it would be to stop in my approach to God and say, "Father that other child of yours, my brother, is indebted to me. I'll be right back as soon as I go take care of that." How can I come into God's presence asking for forgiveness if I can't be forgiving? How much more important is this principle when it comes to being the kind of husband I am to be?

Forgiveness Is Love

First Corinthians 13:4-6 describes the attitude of love as being patient, kind, not envious, not boastful, not rude, not selfish, not easily provoked, keeps no record of wrong, does not rejoice in iniquity but in the truth. How many of these concepts could be achieved by the act of forgiving?

How could we paraphrase Paul to describe the importance of forgiveness as the supreme expression of love? Forgiveness involves patience, kindness, eliminates the jealous attitude of, "Look what I did for you, and what have you done for me?" Forgiveness does not parade its wounds and scars, is not rude, is not selfish and doesn't use old hurts as a reason to get mad easy.

Or let's try the opposite: Unforgiving people are impatient, unkind, jealous of people whom they don't forgive, make a constant display of why they have a right to be hurt or unhappy; they are rude, selfish and easily provoked because of the sensitivity of the "unhealed" hurts.

To be the best husband ever, I don't have to be a perfect man. I just have to start every day with a perfect wife. She was not perfect yesterday. But she was forgiven before I went to sleep. So she started today being perfect. She will not be perfect by the end of the day; but she will be in the morning. Forgiveness does not actually change her, but it changes the way I see her.

HONEY-DO LIST: Item #10
Start Every Day With a Perfect Wife

1. How would your wife rank you as a "forgiving" husband?

   Circle a Number   1 2 3 4 5 6 7 8 9 10 +

2. Why not a lower number?

3. Name three things you could do this week to rank higher in her mind.

4. Which one would most make her feel treasured?

5. How could you go about making this change?

6. What would be the first step?

7. When and where could you begin this week? Be specific. Time? Place?

8. How committed are you to making this change to bring her more joy?

   Circle a Number   1 2 3 4 5 6 7 8 9 10 +

9. If your commitment level is less than a 9, go back to step 3 and be more creative.

Powering Up

Pray for God's help in becoming a Christlike husband by becoming more forgiving. If you will humble yourself, God will lift your marriage up (James 4:10). Shed the pride and enjoy the ride.

Marriage Magic

Plan an overnight trip within easy driving distance. It might be a camping trip with picnics, walking trails, waterfalls and marshmallows by the fire, or it could be a night in the city taking in a concert, Broadway show or inspiring movie. Do not tell your wife where you are going. Surprises restore mystery and fun back to the relationship.

Chapter 11

BE PATIENT
Ben Hayes

It is a daily struggle to keep and build patience.

I love my dad. Always have. We still spend a lot of time together hunting and occasionally hitting the golf course. I talk to him almost every day. It is actually funny when I think about how it was when I was growing up. I remember him as being much less patient than he is today. I remember him having very little patience trying to watch "Monday Night Football" as this goofy kid would grab a football and crash into the couch like he was hitting the defensive line. Turns out, he probably had a whole lot more patience than I realized.

I am now married and have four children, all under the age of 10. I work with a church, I am a counselor, and I help out at a local Christian school. To say that I am stretched thin might be putting it mildly. To say that my patience is strong would be a lie. It is a daily struggle to keep and build patience.

Unfortunately, what I have found both through my own marriage and through my experiences with other couples is that the majority of our impatience is witnessed by, and most of the time directed toward, those we love the most. Sometimes that is our children. Sometimes that is our wives. For some reason our comfort level with our families results in a shorter fuse with them than we have with our church friends or co-workers. Often it is those struggles that we have with people at work and in the community that wear down our patience and leave us raw by the time we get home. The result can be disastrous to a marriage.

God Is Patient

As I read through the Bible, if there is any quality that seems to stand out among the many qualities of God, it seems to be patience. That might surprise some people because of Sodom and Gomorrah, the great flood, Ananias and Sapphira and others. However, even in those stories we see His great patience. Abraham bargained with God about saving Sodom and Gomorrah for a certain number of righteous people found there. Noah preached to the people of the world regarding salvation from the flood for many years. Ananias and Sapphira were allowed the opportunity to tell the truth. Peter reminds us in his second letter, "The Lord is not slack concerning His promise, as some count slackness, but is longsuffering toward us, not willing that any should perish but that all should come to repentance" (2 Peter 3:9).

I wonder if when Peter wrote those words he was thinking of his younger years. Perhaps, especially, the time that he sat upon the beach with the resurrected Christ and had a somewhat frustrating discussion with the Savior. "Simon, son of Jonah, do you love Me?" was asked of Peter three times. Each time, Peter affirmed his love for Jesus, and Jesus replied with an encouragement for Peter to continue the work (John 21:15-17).

What makes this passage significant is that it had only been a few days since Peter had confidently declared, "Lord, I am ready to go with You, both to prison and to death" (Luke 22:33). Jesus assured Peter that the opposite would be true: "I tell you, Peter, the rooster shall not crow this day before you will deny three times that you know Me" (v. 34). A few hours later Peter and Jesus exchanged a glance as the rooster crowed, and Peter was stricken with extreme guilt. He "went out and wept bitterly" (vv. 60-62).

Three times he denied Him in the courtyard. Three times he affirmed his love on the beach after the resurrection. Fewer than 50 days later, he was standing before a crowd of more than 3,000 people talking about the Savior. Peter may have denied Jesus, but our Lord is patient. Peter was just one among many who didn't always get everything exactly right but who served a patient God.

Moses was a fugitive when God called him to return to Egypt and lead the people out of bondage. David committed adultery but is remembered as a man after God's own heart (1 Samuel 13:14; Acts 13:22). Elijah, a great prophet, struggled with his faith on Mount Horeb just days after seeing God completely humiliate the prophets of Baal and Asherah (1 Kings 18-19). In every situation then and now, God is more than patient.

Love Is Patient

What does all this have to do with being the best husband ever?
• God is patient. *We got that.*
• Jesus was patient. *Understood.*
• We are to be like Jesus. *Sure.*
• We are to model the actions of Jesus in our relationships. *Easier said than done.*

"Husbands, love your wives, just as Christ also loved the church" (Ephesians 5:25) is easy to roll off the tongue, but difficult to model in life. When we break down true love in 1 Corinthians 13 we see that "love is patient" (v. 4 ESV). In fact, it is the first quality in a list of many. Why is it listed first? Coincidence? Maybe, but it is also possible that Paul knew it was perhaps the most difficult of all the traits of love. Take care of patience, and you just might breeze through the rest. When you are patient, it is much easier to be kind. When you are patient, envy is not likely to rear its ugly head as often. Most people who are patient aren't rude or self-seeking. A patient love can bear all things.

Programmed for Impatience

You have probably heard that patience is a virtue. However, it is not a virtue that is practiced very often. We are actually programmed in our society to be impatient. We can have it our way at restaurants. Most of us find it mind-numbing if we have to stand in line at Walmart for more than 15 minutes (especially when there are only 4 out of 20 lanes open). If our Internet browser does not open up in less than two seconds, we are calling our provider. Emails are received immediately now because they come to our phone. If we do not get an immediate reply to our instant message, text or email, we wonder what is wrong with the person on the other end of the message. Problems can be worked out in one hour or less on our TV shows. Criminal investigation and forensics are never done in real life as quickly as they make them seem on our favorite crime shows. Do you still think we are not programmed for impatience?

When you look at our homes, it is sometimes not much better. We are unwavering in our expectations and unforgiving in what we want. Some men expect supper on the table at a certain time regardless of what has happened in the home that day. Baby is sick. Doesn't matter; supper is at 5 p.m. sharp. Neighbor needed help. Who cares? Supper is at 5 p.m. sharp. House burned down … Okay, that's an exaggeration. But you get the point.

Practice and Patience

Many times this is a trait that has been passed down from generation to generation. Because we have been programmed in this manner, husbands must be more diligent to grow in their patience. Peter reminded us to give "all diligence" to add many things to our faith. One of those things listed is "perseverance" (2 Peter 1:5-7). I think it is important to understand that this is no simple task. That is why Peter says to make every effort or be diligent. Perseverance and patience take practice. It takes commitment.

So how do we become diligent to grow in our patience? How do we add perseverance to our repertoire? I'm sure it is different for every person, but here are a few suggestions that might help.

Pragmatism and Patience

It is important to begin any endeavor with realistic expectations. Shooting for the moon may land you among the stars when you are setting your personal goals, but setting your expectations too high for things you cannot control may send you crashing down. When reality does not match my expectations in life, I can become discouraged. That quickly robs my bank of patience.

I may seem to be suggesting that you not trust in the abilities of others, but that is not what I am suggesting at all. What I have seen happen on many occasions is for couples to believe everything will be perfect when they slip that ring on each other's fingers. Think about that day in your life. What did you expect? Were there things about marriage, specifically your wife's contribution to marriage, that failed to live up to your expectations? Has it been a source of frustration? The answer is likely yes. Check your expectations. Are they reasonable? If not, adjust.

I have never been a huge fan of roller coasters. I think I finally figured out part of the reason for that: I don't like to give up control. When on a coaster, I can't hit the brakes or adjust my speed. I am at the mercy of the machine and its operator. That's uncomfortable ground for me. What we find in life is that there are many situations where we do not have control. Specifically, I do not have complete control over anyone other than myself. I can persuade or encourage people to do what I want, but ultimately I cannot control them.

If you think about most things that test your patience you will find that it is very similar to being on a roller coaster: the controls are out of your hands. Sunday drivers. Waiters. Lines at Walmart (yes, that's the second time I've mentioned this). Our wives (careful with this one).

I can encourage. I can lovingly ask and persuade. I cannot force her (or anyone else) to do what I want, though. This is not a discussion of what the women are to do and whether they are supposed to be submissive. This is about our response. God has never forced His people to do what He wanted them to do. We have been given free choice. Although He has always had the power to control man, He has allowed freedom. No doubt that has taken a great deal of patience.

Prayer and Patience

How do I become more like God and have His patience in dealing with my wife, kids and life in general? Spend time with God. The people we spend the most time with tend to rub off on us. You have traits that you picked up from your parents or mentors. The people in Acts 4:13 could tell that Peter and John had been with Jesus. I wonder if the people around us notice the same thing.

I have to be honest. I have always been a little scared to pray for patience. I have always heard the warning that if you pray for patience you will likely endure difficult times to help build patience. I don't know if this is true or not. I suppose the best way to build patience is to be put in situations that help you do so, but I'm not sure this is a biblical view. We are not told that Job asked to develop patience before God allowed Satan to torment his physical existence by destroying his possessions and killing his children. David, as far as I can tell, did not ask God to give him patience before he spent years running from King Saul.

I suppose it is possible that God gives us certain situations to test our faith and grow our patience. James encourages us to "count it all joy" when we come against trials of various kinds since the testing of our faith produces patience which helps to make us complete "lacking nothing" (James 1:2-4). The next passage encourages us to ask God for wisdom because He is a God who "gives to all liberally" (v. 5). Will we endure situations that increase the opportunity to grow in patience? Yes. Does God specifically send them when we ask for patience? That I do not know.

I do know this: God blesses us when we seek Him first in all things (Matthew 6:33). So take the time to pray for all the areas of your life that need work and be willing to put those things into practice. Read God's Word. Meditate on the stories of men and women who demonstrated faithful patience in dealing with difficult situations. Ask yourself how you could apply it to your situation, even if your situation appears small compared to the things they were facing. "For whatever things were written before were written for our learning, that we through the patience and comfort of the Scriptures might have hope" (Romans 15:4).

Be patient. Easier said than done, I know. However, as we strive for patience by spending time with the Father and realizing that not all things are under our control, we will find that God will supply us with what we need for each situation. Remember, He is patient and loving toward us, even when we fall short of His glory. We will not always be as patient as we want to be. During those times, remember the lesson Peter learned many years ago on the beach with the resurrected Jesus: God is patient, and He loves you even when you fail. Let's demonstrate that same characteristic with the people we love.

HONEY-DO LIST: Item #11
Be as Patient With Her as Christ Is With Me

1. How would your wife rank you as a "patient" husband?

   Circle a Number   1 2 3 4 5 6 7 8 9 10 +

2. Why not a lower number?

3. Name three things you could do this week to rank higher in her mind.

4. Which one would most make her feel treasured?

5. How could you go about making this change?

6. What would be the first step?

7. When and where could you begin this week? Be specific. Time? Place?

8. How committed are you to making this change to bring her more joy?

   Circle a Number   1 2 3 4 5 6 7 8 9 10 +

9. If your commitment level is less than a 9, go back to step 3 and be more creative.

Powering Up

Pray for God's help in becoming a Christlike husband by becoming more patient. Withholding love to get love is ineffective and irrational. Imagine how things will improve when your first instinct is to give your wife what she needs instead of calculating what she deserves.

Marriage Magic

Where has your wife always wanted to go for dinner? Find out and make a reservation this week. Make it an evening to remember. Open her door, hold her hand, pull out her chair, gaze into her eyes. For this night, leave the cell phone in your pocket (except to take a picture). This is her night with the man of her dreams. Make it special.

Chapter 12

BE PRAYERFUL
Aubrey Johnson

*What would you pray for your wife and family
if you knew it was your last day on earth?*

The Olympics are a global celebration of human potential. The contests themselves are meaningless, but the world is wonderstruck by the way elite athletes push their minds and bodies to the limit. Society is not altered for good or evil by shaving a tenth of a second off a world record, but people are inspired by what you can do with focus and commitment.

If there were a spiritual Olympics and you could choose one event to enter, what would it be? How about becoming a prayer Olympian? Imagine how your life would be altered if you pushed yourself to pray more and better. What if you specialized in praying for your mate and your marriage? To become the best husband you can be, nothing will accelerate your progress more than praying like Jesus.

Jesus' ministry was bathed in prayer from start to finish. At the outset, He was praying when the heavens opened, the Spirit descended and God claimed Him as His Son (Luke 3:21-22). At the conclusion, His final words were gasps of prayer from the cross. Jesus was a man of determined prayer, and many of those prayers were on behalf of His bride, the church.

Romantically inclined, men boast that they would swim the deepest ocean, cross the widest river or climb the highest mountain for their sweethearts. That is impressive, but true love demands something even greater. Would you get down on your knees for her? Not on a solitary occasion like a proposal, but take to your knees every day on her behalf. Jesus crossed the gulf between heaven and earth to save His bride, but He also bowed low in prayer to carry her back to the throne of God.

When you wake up, get down on your knees and pray for God's help to become the best husband ever. Ask Him to help you make her feel treasured, avoid bringing pain into her life, and make it a banner day in her time upon the earth.

In addition to praying for your wife, be sure to spend time praying with her. When we were younger, I started holding Lisa's hand during prayer times at worship. In the beginning, it was occasional and spontaneous. At some point, I realized that this was a precious way to show my love for Lisa and the Lord at the same time. Holding her hand became not mechanical but intentional. Now I cherish the moments when we squeeze each other's hand during public prayers. It was a practice that became a habit that became a joy. Happy marriages are bound together with small gestures of affection and respect. What are your private ways of saying, "You mean the world to me"?

Pray Attention

Prayer is not the whole answer to a fulfilling marriage, but it is more important than you think. Prayer is God's means of keeping first things first in a life crowded with competing interests. What do you want more of in your life, and how do you go about getting it? The answer is simple: You must pray attention.

The biggest threat facing your marriage is worldly distractions. A distraction is something that keeps you from giving your full attention to what is most important at the moment. In the parable of the sower (Matthew 13), Jesus compared life's distractions to thorns. Thorns are mental weeds that divert your attention and deplete your energy. They grow quickly and can overtake your best plans. When other people's agendas encroach on your goals, you are battling dangerous weeds.

So how do you battle the weeds of distraction that keep you from remembering the purpose of marriage and practicing ways to express your love? How do you focus your mind on your most important goals to keep them from fading into the background? By praying attention.

Prayer is a divine means of collecting and directing your thoughts to increase their power. It links your mind to your highest aspirations. It strengthens commitment and sparks creativity. When you pray to God about your marriage, you cannot help but think of new ways to show your love to your wife. A holy chain of events flows from filling your mind with thoughts of her, and God could not be more pleased.

Pray First, Play Later

Prayer can also help you make better decisions, especially when you are under pressure. My friend Joe Henry was a sailor on the USS Saratoga. One day while the ship was in port, he got a phone message from his wife, Kathy, asking him to come home early because she needed help. After an abbreviated workday, he was headed home when some buddies asked him to join them in a round of golf. After a brief hesitation, he decided he would. Why not? He would get home at the usual time, and no one would be the wiser.

When retrieving his clubs from his car, he did not notice his key slip off the key ring and quietly fall into the trunk. Slamming the lid, he was off for an afternoon of fun with the boys. When they concluded the round, he returned to his car but could not find his key. Sheepishly, he called his wife and asked her to come rescue him. Worst of all, his car was at the golf club and not the naval base.

Kathy drove 40 miles to help Joe on a day when it was inconvenient even though he would not come home to assist her when he had leisure time on his hands. Looking back on that day, Joe knows a moment of prayer and a better decision could have saved him a lot of regret and embarrassment. Prayer puts things in perspective so you can make choices that honor God and your highest commitments. When you fail to pray, you are more likely to make impulsive decisions that undermine your priorities and your integrity. So what is more important: Your handicap or your home life?

Prayers for Presley

Few things make your wife feel more respect and affection for you than praying for your children. When you care for them, you care for her. The week before his first child was born, our youth minister shared

this prayer list for his daughter. He prayed that she will:
- dream bigger than I and that I will let her dream
- not have to do great things based on my plans but can have her own
- love the church and see the love of the church in us
- glory in the cross and not her own accomplishments
- want wisdom and understanding, not just to be right
- grow through discouragement and fight through failures
- have a tender heart and cry for things worth crying over
- not look down on others but be quick to confess her sins and mistakes
- know what marriage should be like from watching us
- marry an amazing man (like her daddy) who will help her get to heaven
- love that husband more than me and God more than him

Your prayers for your child may not be as poignant as this, but they can be just as powerful. Imagine what would happen if you prayed the same three things for your son or daughter every morning and night for 21 years? The mere fact that you are thinking of your child is monumental. Desiring the best for your child and verbalizing it in positive language is huge. Good things flow from the simplest of prayers. No matter what, just pray.

The Greatest Prayer Ever Prayed

In an upper room, on the night of His arrest, Jesus spent His final hours of freedom preparing the apostles for the challenges before them. John 17 records the memorable prayer He prayed on behalf of His followers. It was a passionate plea for God to bless His bride, the church.

That raises a serious question: What would you pray for your wife and family if you knew it was your last day on earth? Maybe those are the things you should be praying before you reach the end of your life (or the end of your marriage). Unlike Jesus, no man knows for sure when his hour will come (Matthew 24:36), but prayer will help you be ready when that moment arrives. These topics were on Jesus' mind as He lifted His eyes to heaven.

What Jesus Prayed for His Bride

• **Faithfulness** – "Keep through Your name those whom You have given Me" (John 17:11).

Christian husbands should pray tirelessly for God's help in strength-ening the faith of their families. To be "kept" in God's name (v. 12) is to remain faithful to Him through the means He provides to save and sanctify His people. Through faith in Christ and obedience to His will, Christians identify themselves as belonging to God. To help them stay faithful, God has gone to extraordinary lengths. He provided the New Testament to guide them in making choices that abound in blessings. He established the church to teach them His will and help them live it. He gave them shepherds to feed their spirits and watch over their souls. When they go astray, He has provided a path back and an Advo-cate to intercede for them. And He gave your family to you. Will you give yourself up to present them to Christ in splendor without "spot or wrinkle or any such thing" (Ephesians 5:27)? Pray God will help you help them keep the faith once delivered unto the saints (Jude 1:3).

• **Joy** – "I come to You ... that they may have My joy fulfilled in themselves" (John 17:13).

The reason Jesus left His disciples and returned to heaven was to bless them in greater measure. He gave up His earthy life so that they could have eternal life and a more joyful life. Everything He did was for their good. Likewise, a Christlike husband puts the welfare of his family before his personal concerns. The joy of his family is more important than his own comfort or pleasure. Long-term joy is the aim of a Christian husband: The kind that is deep, lasting and holy. When you ask God to help you bring more joy into the lives of your wife and children, it delights your Father and your family. The gospel of Jesus is a joy-producing message and Christians are joy-producing people. By definition then, a Christlike husband is in the joy creation business. Praying like Jesus will make you a channel of Christ's joy.

• **Safety** – "Keep them from the evil one" (John 17:15).

How seriously do you take your job of caring for your spouse's safety? When you married, protecting your mate and marriage became one of your top responsibilities. The evil one is bent on turning your happy home into a sad statistic. Should you beat the odds and stay together, he still wants your wife's soul for his morbid collection. So what are you doing about it? One thing is for sure: You are no match for the devil on your own. So why not ask God to join the battle with you? Jesus guarded His followers using prayer as a critical part of His defense strategy. Worldly friends and shameless celebrities are intent on pulling your loved ones into their web of ungodly living. False teachers and self-promoters work from within the church to steal the hearts of the unwary. You cannot take your family out of the world, but you can teach, warn, encourage and, by all means, pray for them (Ephesians 6:18).

• **Growth** – "Sanctify them by Your truth" (John 17:17).

Salvation is one source of joy in a Christian's life (Acts 8:39). Another is spiritual growth. The word "sanctify" means to set apart. The more your thoughts, words and deeds are distinctively Christian, the better your life will be. Sanctification is a result of loving and living God's Word. If your wife and children are to be sanctified, you must become God's vessel to bring more of Christ's truth to their lives. How? You could read the Bible to your family at mealtimes; conduct family devotionals once a week; make sure they get to church assemblies on time, rested and ready to engage; ask questions about what they learned and how they will apply it; and create opportunities for them to be around Christian friends and role models. Most of all, you must bring God's truth to their lives through your example. Do your speech, attitude and choices promote their spiritual growth? The key to their growth is your growth. Become a man of the Word, and you will become a catalyst for your family's spiritual growth.

• **Heaven** – "I desire that they … may be with Me where I am, that they may behold My glory" (John 17:24).

Separation can be painful, even temporary separation. When you are on a business trip, your thoughts turn to home. You count the days till you will be reunited with your loved ones. When your children leave for college, you look forward to calls and weekend visits. When they are grown and on their own, you cannot wait for holidays and reunions. The desire for togetherness is great. But how much more should Christians want to be with their families in eternity? Jesus used the word "desire" to describe His yearning to be surrounded by His disciples in heaven (John 17:24). "Desire" refers to a strong feeling of wanting. It is something you think about continuously and organize your life around. It guides your choices and drives your behavior. Above every earthly concern is this supreme goal: We are going to be together in heaven.

We are going to see Jesus and share in His glory. If nothing is more important, then no prayer request is more vital. It will keep you and your loved ones from being distracted by temptations or discouraged by trials. The more you pray about heaven, the more you think of heaven, and the more you think about heaven, the more you live for heaven.

Pray Through Pain

Leaving the upper room, Jesus made His way to Gethsemane. In the garden, Jesus prayed, "Let this cup pass from Me" (Matthew 26:39). When going through painful marital problems, it is not wrong to ask God to "let this cup pass." Still, it is best to close as He did by adding, "Not my will, but Yours be done" (Luke 22:42). If a measure of pain is necessary to produce positive outcomes, so be it. Facing the pain may be exactly what is needed for healing and progress. Frankly, a man who is not willing to carry a cross has no business getting married.

Jesus accepted God's will and modified His prayers accordingly. In His prayer on the cross, He asked, "Father, forgive them, for they do not know what they do" (Luke 23:34). Can you pray these words on behalf of your spouse when something she says or does causes you pain? When you feel misjudged or attacked, remember how the best husband ever responded. He prayed and forgave. Your wife may wound you inadvertently, but sympathy is more appropriate than anger, and prayer is more fitting than payback. Do not succumb to the pain, pray your way through the pain.

Pray Your Future

Frederick Buechner said, "Go where your best prayers take you." Jesus' best prayers led Him to the cross and then to glory. At the cross, He gave His best to save His bride. In glory, He is preparing His best for her. The welfare of the church was the constant theme of Christ's best prayers.

So what about you? What are you passionately praying for? Where will your best prayers take you? Into the heart of your spouse? Into the lives of your children? To God's throne with your family? You cannot lead them where your prayers do not lead you. Pray as if their lives depend on it – because they do.

HONEY-DO LIST: Item #12
Get on My Knees for Her Every Morning

1. How would your wife rank you as a "prayerful" husband?

   Circle a Number   1 2 3 4 5 6 7 8 9 10 +

2. Why not a lower number?

3. Name three things you could do this week to rank higher in her mind.

4. Which one would most make her feel treasured?

5. How could you go about making this change?

6. What would be the first step?

7. When and where could you begin this week? Be specific. Time? Place?

8. How committed are you to making this change to bring her more joy?

   Circle a Number   1 2 3 4 5 6 7 8 9 10 +

9. If your commitment level is less than a 9, go back to step 3 and be more creative.

Powering Up

"The fervent prayer of a righteous man avails much" (James 5:16). How passionately have you been praying for your marriage? Ask for God's help in becoming a Christlike husband by praying persistently for your wife and family. A righteous man is one who lives like he prays.

Marriage Magic

This week, find a place where you both feel comfortable praying. Thank God for the gift of someone to love and with whom to share His love. Thank Him for someone whose love has made you feel special and capable. Talk with God about your difficulties, dreams and destiny.

A Christlike Husband's
HOPE

---

*"Having loved His own who were
in the world,
He loved them to the end"*
(John 13:1).

When the deepest desire of your heart is to
bless your wife every day of your life, you have
discovered the door to true intimacy. Committed
love is the cornerstone of great relationships.
Therefore, to win your wife's heart, your love
must be steadfast. John wrote these words about
Jesus' unwavering devotion: "Having loved His
own who were in the world, He loved them to
the end" (John 13:1). Is your love trustworthy?
Risk-worthy? Hope-worthy? Chapter 13 will
explain how a "7:12 mindset" can keep you
from losing your wife's confidence by maintaining your commitment to becoming the best
husband ever.

THE 7:12 MINDSET
Aubrey Johnson

Your happiness in life is limited only by your ability to imagine more ways of bringing joy to others.

The purpose of this final chapter is to help you live the best husband ever challenge going forward. A challenge is something that tests your abilities. It implies that an undertaking is difficult but worth the effort. It hints at the deep satisfaction you will experience when you overcome obstacles and realize your goal with the help of Christ (Philippians 4:13).

So here is the final challenge. Once you finish this book and set it aside, how will you keep your commitment to grow more Christlike as a husband? It is easy to relapse and fall into old patterns of behavior that are comfortable but selfish. To move forward will require a permanent change in your thinking. It requires a *7:12 Mindset*.

The *Golden Rule*

In Matthew 7:12, Jesus shared His most powerful tool for living an abundant life. The Golden Rule, as it is more commonly known, is also the world's most effective tool for improving your marriage. Jesus said, "Therefore, whatever you want men to do to you, do also to them, for this is the Law and the Prophets." Imagine that – all the wisdom of the Old Testament boiled down into one all-purpose tool. The Golden Rule is not one teaching among many, but the foundational principle of all biblical teachings. If you understand and apply this simple rule, it will take your spiritual life and relationships to a whole new level.

The word "whatever" suggests that the *7:12 Mindset* works in a broad set of circumstances. Its usefulness is not restricted to narrow applications in specific conditions. You can apply it at work, in child-rearing, in building friendships, or in dealing with difficult people. Best of all, it works like magic in your marriage.

The more empathy you develop, the better your relationship with your wife. When you not only see her situation but also feel her feelings, you are instantly drawn closer and the way forward becomes clearer. The path becomes plain when you look at her with your heart and not just your head.

You do not have to be a professional therapist to solve most relational problems. No degree, certification or specialized knowledge is needed. Choosing the best course forward is simple: Just put yourself in the other person's shoes and ask how you would like to be treated. In this case, put yourself in your wife's shoes and take a spin around the room. Look at the world through her eyes for a minute. Imagine if you had her responsibilities resting on your shoulders. Feel the weight of her pressures and problems. Consider her desires and dreams, and imagine if you had to deal with you.

Let it be clear, though, that the blessings are in the doing (James 1:22). Actions always trump intentions (2:14-17). The purpose of thinking is to act, and the purpose of Christian thinking is to act lovingly (1 John 3:18). When couples are not satisfied with the treatment they are receiving from each other, they can affectionately ask, "Was that a *7:12 Mindset*?" When you say it with a smile, this playful reminder may be all it takes to get things back on track.

Imagination Therapy

The Golden Rule teaches you to harness the power of your imagination. Sadly, many use their imaginations for unholy and destructive purposes. In Noah's day, God destroyed the earth because of mankind's wickedness. In describing the extent of man's depravity, Genesis 6:5 says that, "every imagination of the thoughts of his heart was only evil continually" (KJV).

How you think determines your character, quality of life and eternal destiny. It also determines the future of your marriage. You can spend your energy resenting your wife and considering how to manipulate or punish her, or you can spend your time imagining how to bless and bring happiness to her. Think solutions, not exit strategies.

All people have imaginations, but spiritual people have sanctified imaginations. Their thoughts are influenced more by the Spirit than the flesh. They take control of their thinking and channel it toward constructive, God-honoring actions. Even new Christians can do this. From the moment of conversion, the imagination shifts its attention from satisfying self to serving others.

An Illustration

To illustrate the *7:12 Mindset*, envision a box that represents your thinking. On the left side are thoughts about you and on the right side are thoughts about your spouse. Now draw a horizontal line through the middle of the box. On the bottom half are negative thoughts and on the top half are positive thoughts. At this point, the box is divided into four quadrants that represent four categories of thinking. Am I thinking more about her or myself? Are my thoughts predominantly positive or negative? Everyone spends more time in one of these quadrants than the others. This becomes your default way of thinking or mindset.

Which box is best?	Me-First Thoughts	Her-First Thoughts
Positive Thoughts	Delusion	Delight
Negative Thoughts	Discouragement	Disparagement

The question is, which quadrant is best for improving your marriage? Everyone spends some time in each of these areas, but is one way of thinking more beneficial than the others? By becoming aware of which quadrant you are in, you can understand why you feel and behave as you do. If you do not like what that thinking produces in your life, you can shift your thoughts to a more desirable quadrant. Through self-awareness and diligent practice, anyone can develop a *7:12 Mindset*.

Me-First Thoughts

Box 1 – Minimizing Your Strengths (Proverbs 17:22)

When your thoughts are centered on you in a negative way, the result is discouragement. You may think you see yourself realistically, but your pessimism has distorted your viewpoint. Your mental filter causes you to discount your good qualities and minimize your good deeds. You give greater weight to your imperfections and blow them out of proportion. The effect of this internal nit-picking is insecurity and a broken spirit. Trust me, you are not much fun to be around when you constantly think this way.

Box 2 – Minimizing Your Weaknesses (Romans 12:3)

Self-esteem is a good thing, but egotism (obsession with yourself) is a bad thing. It reduces your concern for others and makes you conceited. Positive feelings about yourself are beneficial when you are humble and when they are balanced by concern for others. However, thinking of yourself first and most is a problem. The effect of this kind of self-centered thinking is vanity and insensitivity. When you think too much of yourself, the result can be delusion.

Her-First Thoughts

Box 3 – Maximizing Her Weaknesses (Matthew 7:1)

When your thoughts are centered on others in a negative way, the result is disparagement. In this quadrant, most of your thinking is critical. You spend your time judging and condemning others. When your thinking is stuck in this area, you can always find something about your spouse that disappoints you. Consequently, you spend much of your time feeling frustrated, angry and superior. You are also destined to feel lonely because few people are drawn to a person who is constantly finding fault. Solomon wrote that it is the glory of a man "to overlook a transgression" (Proverbs 19:11).

A critic cannot understand why people do not appreciate his advice because it is meant to benefit them. Believing his intentions are good and his criticism constructive, he continues a pattern of negative behavior that alienates him from family members. The effect of a judgmental spirit is condescension or contempt for others. It is an unloving outlook that ignores people's feelings and undervalues their worth. Peter said, "Love will cover a multitude of sins" (1 Peter 4:8).

Box 4 – Maximizing Her Strengths (1 Corinthians 13:7)

When your thoughts are focused on her in a positive way, the result is pure delight. It is a win-win situation for everyone involved. She likes it better, and you feel better about yourself. What man does not want quadrant-four thinking from his spouse? According to Jesus, if that is what you want from her then that is what you should do for her.

This is the great commandment zone where you value her strengths rather than disparage her weaknesses and assume her motives are honorable even when you think her behavior is questionable. It is the zone of other-mindedness (Matthew 22:37-39; Philippians 2:3). Her interests and welfare take precedence over your ego and agenda. The result is closeness, less conflict and better communication. When this is your default outlook, you become more thankful and more joyful.

Practicing Praise

Living appreciatively is the key to a better marriage and a better life. It begins with choosing to notice more good things than bad things (you find what you look for in most cases). It is reinforced by telling her what you notice and appreciate. Never keep appreciation to yourself. When you share it, you encourage her, but you also strengthen your habit of seeing the good. Her smiles will make you glad you did. The more compassionate and kind you are, the healthier and happier your relationship will be.

Here is a suggestion: Begin and end every day by telling her something you appreciate about her. Where did she sacrifice or go the extra mile? What character trait do you admire or what kind deed has she done? Her faults are easy to spot and tempting to criticize, but negativity is a nail in the coffin of any relationship. If harping does not help, why do it? She is more likely to change spontaneously when she knows you appreciate her efforts to please you. However few or small those gestures may be, notice and praise them and they will multiply.

The advantages of a you-first mindset are obvious, especially when both parties are on board. If both partners think self-first, joy is rare; if one partner is selfish and the other is unselfish, joy is occasional; but when a husband and wife are both thinking unselfishly and positively about each other, joy is as regular as the rising of the sun. This was God's ideal for marriage: Consistent, predictable selfless love. When Adam and Eve allowed selfish thinking to enter their relationship, their marriage suffered. The same is true today. The good news is that Jesus came not only to redeem your soul but to restore your home to God's original plan.

Encouraging Change

"You mean I should never tell her of a change I would like her to make?" No, of course not, but watch your timing and tone (Proverbs 27:15). I recommend a 14-to-1 ratio of praise to petitions for change. Once a week is probably pushing it, and once a month may be best. Frankly, it depends on the health of your relationship. When trust is low, less is more. When she is convinced you have her best interests at heart, addressing interpersonal issues will become natural and spontaneous.

When you broach the subject, do not focus on what you dislike ("Do you know what really bugs me?"). Practice telling her what you want without being critical ("Do you know what makes me really feel loved?"). Invitations feel much nicer than demands. Done right, requests sound like opportunities rather than attacks.

Also, be sure to match her effort. Ask her to tell you something you could change to please her. When she sees you are working as hard on the relationship as she is, it creates natural motivation to try harder. If both of you acknowledge each others' efforts and progress, there are no limits to how satisfying your marriage can become.

Overcoming Resentment

"But what if she is not pulling her weight?" Most men believe their wives are not putting equal effort into the relationship. Why? Because they have become skilled at collecting evidence in support of their conclusion. It keeps them from feeling bad for doing so little themselves. The real problem is the mindset. It keeps you from noticing the good things she does. Challenge your thinking, and you will begin to see what you were overlooking. The Lord said, "You will seek Me and find Me, when you search for Me with all your heart" (Jeremiah 29:13). Likewise, you will find your wife's love when you search for it with all your heart. By searching for her good qualities, you will discover a wonderful person waiting to be known and loved.

"But supposing it is true – if she is not pulling her weight, what then?" This is where Christians have a big advantage in producing positive change. Rather than waiting for signs that you are appreciated and that your efforts are reciprocated, just go first. When Jesus gathered His disciples in an upper room, no one offered to wash His feet. What did Jesus do? He washed their feet. Remember, Jesus did not say, "Whatever men do to you, do also to them." Instead, He said, "Whatever you want men to do to you, do also to them" (Matthew 7:12). There is a difference. Your behavior is not based on their actions but on your aspirations. Be the change you want to see in your marriage.

If you want a wonderful marriage, sow seeds in keeping with what you want to harvest (Galatians 6:7). Planting ragweed will not produce roses, and exchanging insults will never produce intimacy. The urge to criticize may be the greatest temptation you ever face. To defeat this unholy habit, you must realize that the problem is with your heart, not your sweetheart.

In most cases, when you consistently act the way you want to be treated, she will eventually respond in kind. If not, you will still like yourself better and you will have the peace of mind that comes from knowing you tried your best (Romans 12:17-18). This is the Christian way: The way of love (1 Corinthians 12:31).

HONEY-DO LIST: Item #13

Develop a 7:12 Mindset

1. What is a "challenge"?

2. What was challenging about the best husband ever challenge?

3. What is a *7:12 Mindset*?

4. Do you need special training to solve marriage problems?

5. How is the imagination a tool for improving your marriage?

6. How do some husbands misuse their imaginations?

7. Why is choosing to live appreciatively a good idea?

8. Why is it important to share what you appreciate?

9. Why is the urge to criticize such a great temptation?

10. How does the law of sowing and reaping apply to marriage?

Power Up

At the beginning of each day, get down on your knees and ask God to help you become the best husband ever. Pray for your wife's well-being and for new ways to make her feel treasured.

Marriage Magic

Now that you have finished the book, how will you keep moving forward with the skills you've learned? Brainstorm three ways you will strive to become the best husband ever after the class is over. Write them down, discuss them, and add them to your calendar. Why not make this an annual practice every Feb. 14?

Conclusion

What have you learned from this study? How has it changed you? How has it changed your marriage? Who will you bless by sharing a copy of this book?

AFTERWORD

Aubrey Johnson

In Luke 6:37, Jesus provided a detailed explanation of the Golden Rule. He began by stating the principle negatively: "Judge not, and you shall not be judged. Condemn not, and you shall not be condemned." Judging your spouse leads to condemning your spouse; and when you are judgmental and critical of her, she will be judgmental and critical of you.

Instead of judging and criticizing, be eager to forgive. Jesus said, "Forgive, and you will be forgiven" (Luke 6:37). Withholding forgiveness is shortsighted for two reasons. First, it keeps you trapped in negativity and that does not feel very good. Second, it provokes resentment and retaliation. When you refuse to move on, she feels justified in withholding forgiveness from you. Now everyone is stuck in bitterness until someone decides to get off the merry-go-round of discontent.

If she attempts to repair the relationship, receive it graciously. If she does not, then you go first. When you choose to forgive, you immediately feel better, but so does she. Judgment provokes judgment, but grace evokes grace. When she no longer has to defend herself, she is less invested in hurting you.

So look at this process in detail. Do not judge and condemn because it will only produce a backlash. Instead, forgive her and love her more than ever. If you want love, give love. "Give, and it will be given to you" (Luke 6:38). Give what? Whatever you would want in her circumstance: Forgiveness? Kindness? Understanding?

When you opt to forgive and love again, you cannot hold anything back. Half-measures will not work. If she senses any reluctance, it can make things worse rather than better. Doubting your sincerity can become a habit that makes it twice as hard to reconcile in the future.

How much love should you give? "Good measure, pressed down, shaken together, running over, will be put into your lap. For with the measure you use it will be measured back to you" (Luke 6:38 ESV). The measure matters. The more you give, the more you receive. Conversely, the less you give, the less you receive. The key to a happy marriage is to give more rather than less, and when you think you have given your all, reach down and give some more (2 Corinthians 9:8).

When you give sparingly, it is a big mistake. Testing the waters with your toe and then waiting to see how she responds is a slow and painful path to recovery. The inch-by-inch method is fraught with danger because you are bargaining for love. It is based on scorekeeping, which invites more judging which inevitably leads to condemning. It says you doubt whether things will really improve. The motive has less to do with reconciliation than self-justification ("See, I tried"). Instead, dive in head first. The water may be icy, but things nearly always warm up. Where love abounds, relationships rebound (Philippians 1:9; 1 Thessalonians 3:12).

God wants to pour His best blessings out to you. Pouring refers to a rapid constant flow (not a drip). He wants you to experience love and joy running over (Psalm 23:5). The secret to receiving God's best in your marriage is to give your best. If you are not receiving what you want, there is a reason. Do a self-check to determine the truth about yourself. What you are receiving may be what you are giving. It might be unintentional, but is it possible?

In most cases, you get out of marriage what you put into it. Your looks, tone, words and actions create a response in your mate. If you have a life full of pain and problems, there may be a hidden stream of unpleasant feelings at the source. Could she be hurting you because she is hurting? Could you be the originating source of your own pain?

Jesus said, "The truth shall make you free" (John 8:32). The truth about marriage is that you generally receive what you give in the measure you give. Embracing these truths will free you from the denial and blame that keep you from moving forward in life. It hurts to face these facts, but once your heart is pricked, the healing begins and the blessings flow. The stream of love works like this: It flows from God's heart to yours, from your heart to hers, and from her heart back to you. To receive love, you must give love. To receive much, you must give much. Let the pouring begin.

> *"He who believes in Me,*
> *as the Scripture has said,*
> *out of his heart will flow*
> *rivers of living water."*
> *(John 7:38)*

HONEY-DO LIST

- ○ Take the best husband ever pledge.
- ○ Carry a cross for her, not just a torch.
- ○ Love her like Christ loves her.
- ○ Die to self to start living.
- ○ Make helpfulness a habit.
- ○ Give her grace, not grief.
- ○ Make a daily sacrifice for her.
- ○ Make her my best friend.
- ○ Give her support, not stress.
- ○ Start every day with a perfect wife.
- ○ Be as patient with her as Christ is with me.
- ○ Get on my knees for her every morning.
- ○ Develop a *7:12 Mindset* (Golden Rule).

ABOUT the AUTHORS

Aubrey Johnson

Aubrey Johnson preaches for the Peachtree City Church of Christ near Atlanta, Ga. He is the author of nine books on Christian living and conducts "Dynamic Deacons" and "Effective Elders" seminars for churches of Christ. Aubrey specializes in accentuating the practical benefits of simple New Testament Christianity. He is married to the former Lisa Hearn, and they have three sons.

Cecil May Jr.

Cecil May Jr. serves as dean emeritus of the V.P. Black College of Biblical Studies at Faulkner University in Montgomery, Ala. Before his work in Christian higher education, he was a preacher in Mississippi. He began preaching while a student at Harding University in June 1951. He lectures extensively, writes regularly for several publications, including the *Gospel Advocate*, and holds workshops, seminars and gospel meetings.

He is married to the former Winnie Williamson; they have four children: Betty Lozada, Cecil May III, Roslyn Miller and Richard May. All are faithful Christians. Both sons are preachers and one daughter is married to a preacher. Cecil and Winnie have five grandchildren.

Lonnie Jones

Lonnie Jones is married to Jacque Jones, and they have adventured together for the last 31 years. They are partners in Christianity and friends in the truest sense of the word. Lonnie is a licensed professional counselor with 18 years in private practice. He has been active in full-time or part-time ministry for the last 35-plus years. In addition to the ministry and counseling, Lonnie works as an experience-based learning facilitator and manages the challenge course he designed and constructed for Wellstone Behavioral Services. As a longtime resident of Huntsville, Ala., Lonnie is one of several volunteer police chaplains and has been assigned to the SWAT team for the last 24 years.

Ben Hayes

Ben Hayes serves as a minister of the Highland Park Church of Christ in Muscle Shoals, Ala., and has a private practice as a licensed professional counselor. He holds a bachelor's degree in Bible from Freed-Hardeman University and an educational specialist degree in counseling from the University of Alabama. Ben has been married to his wife, Kenya, since 2002, and they have four children: Jackson, Destin, Branslee and Stana.

www.ingramcontent.com/pod-product-compliance
Lightning Source LLC
LaVergne TN
LVHW021359080426
835508LV00020B/2353